'*How to Understand Your Gender* is a thoughtful, intersectional, embodied invitation to reflect on gender. It has something to offer to readers at every stage of their gender journey, and is a valuable tool for educators and clinicians.'

– *Zena Sharman, PhD, editor of* The Remedy: Queer and Trans Voices on Health *and* Health Care and Persistence: All Ways Butch and Femme

'The authors have made adequate time for Indigenous and Two Spirit identities and people. Talking about decolonising the gender narrative in a way that traces back to the very roots of the first peoples of a place is something that is crucial in providing understanding, but is often ignored or overlooked. Hands down, I will recommend this book for anybody looking to learn more about gender and sexuality. It's an amazing resource for *all*, regardless of identity, experience, or knowledge. I fell head over heels with this book, and I can't wait to shout it from the rooftops!'

– *Katrina Werchouski, Director of Indigenous Cultures Center, Northland College*

'If you want to finally discard the narrow confines of gender and sexuality and explore the vast landscapes of gender and sexual imagination, this is your book!'

– *Jayashree George, DA, ATR-BC, LMFT, lecturer, School of the Art Institute of Chicago*

HOW TO UNDERSTAND
YOUR GENDER

of related interest

The Gender Agenda
A First-Hand Account of How Girls and
Boys Are Treated Differently
Ros Ball and James Millar
Foreword by Marianne Grabrucker
ISBN 978 1 78592 320 3
eISBN 978 1 78450 633 9

Trans Voices
Becoming Who You Are
Declan Henry
Foreword by Professor Stephen Whittle
ISBN 978 1 78592 240 4
eISBN 978 1 78450 520 2

Are You a Boy or Are You a Girl?
Sarah Savage and Fox Fisher
ISBN 978 1 78592 267 1
eISBN 978 1 78450 556 1

Can I tell you about Gender Diversity?
A guide for friends, family and professionals
CJ Atkinson
Illustrated by Olly Pike
ISBN 978 1 78592 105 6
eISBN 978 1 78450 367 3

Who Are You?
The Kid's Guide to Gender Identity
Brook Pessin-Whedbee
Illustrated by Naomi Bardoff
ISBN 978 1 78592 728 7
eISBN 978 1 78450 580 6

HOW TO UNDERSTAND
YOUR GENDER

A Practical Guide for Exploring Who You Are

ALEX IANTAFFI AND MEG-JOHN BARKER

Foreword by S. Bear Bergman

Jessica Kingsley *Publishers*
London and Philadelphia

First published in 2018
by Jessica Kingsley Publishers
73 Collier Street
London N1 9BE, UK
and
400 Market Street, Suite 400
Philadelphia, PA 19106, USA

www.jkp.com

Library of Congress Cataloging in Publication Data
A CIP catalog record for this book is available from the Library of Congress

British Library Cataloguing in Publication Data
A CIP catalogue record for this book is available from the British Library

ISBN 978 1 78592 746 1
eISBN 978 1 78450 517 2

Printed and bound by CPI Group (UK) Ltd, Croydon, CR0 4YY

This book is dedicated to gender pioneers, rebels, and warriors across time and space. Thank you. We are not the first and we won't be the last.

Contents

Foreword

S. Bear Bergman

It has been a few years since I have had the experience I am about to describe, but I don't imagine it will seem unfamiliar or surprising to any transgender/non-binary/genderqueer person: I filled out a ream of forms and submitted them, and received a letter instructing me to present myself on a particular date and time, for purposes of evaluation. The language related to the evaluation varies, depending on time and place, cultural or economic power, but the purpose of the evaluation is constant: 'Today we will find out who you think you are, and we will determine whether we believe your answer can be trusted.'

Whether any individual's answers can be trusted by the gatekeeping medical establishment will be determined using a matrix that seems scientific, but isn't. In fact, it's an audition of respectability; the more 'respectable' you seem to your interlocutor – the more middle class, the more nicely-groomed, the more clean and sober, the more theoretical, the more composed and controlled – then the more likely you are to be believed and therefore approved of.

If you are well able to rise to a single occasion and give the expected answers, the more likely you are to be approved of. There is no aggregate score – no one is keeping track of your cumulative performance – it's now or never, today with this stranger or not at all. Being approved of is the goal. Being disapproved (or disproved) is the blow that ricochets you back beyond the gates to try again, elsewhere, someday. Maybe.

(The narrative is familiar even to people who have never agonized over the right outfit and hairstyle for one of these meetings; like Madge, we are soaking in it. We all know, even those of us who don't know first-hand, that trans and genderqueer and non-binary people's gender identities are always subject to scrutiny, always revocable, and always, always suspect. Don't believe me? Then why do you think the first question any trans person gets asked upon disclosure is, 'Have you had the surgery yet?' What is that but a question of further investigation, an opportunity for a stranger to arrogate to themselves the right to decide if they think you're really trans or not? If you really deserve the pronouns or name or respect you have asserted; if your transition is sufficient for their purposes? The fact that they know absolutely fuck-all about transness and are an adjunct lecturer in mathematics or a librarian or a dental hygienist or a tenth grader gives them zero seconds of pause about whether they really know enough to be interrogating. Trust me.)

For most of the last 75 North American years, that has been our method for welcoming people into a space of medical transition. First the paperwork, then the audition, and then, if you're good (as in, if you've 'been good', in the way of vice principals and your dourest auntie), and you've been lucky, some access. But gosh oh golly, it has not always been this way. It can be difficult to tell people how much it has not always been this way. All of our modern memory about trans people begins with the Center for Transexuality and Dr Harry Benjamin. Frequently I'm asked, 'Why did there start being trans people right around World War II?' or, 'What did trans people do before they could have surgery?' These lines of questioning are always very alarming to me, even though it's perfectly reasonable that people might not know.

They wouldn't know, of course, because all of that information has been systematically, purposefully, and quite violently erased. Colonization took it, and wadded it into a small ball and (literally, actually, as Balboa did in Panama) fed it to a dog – those who resisted conversion were killed, and Christianity, as practiced in the time, had no room at all for anyone beyond the gender binary of male and female, even though prior to colonization many, many indigenous societies had neutral-to-positive words, social roles, and legal standards for people we might today name as transgender in some way. So there's a giant whistling void in our history across large swaths of the world, a void which might otherwise have yielded hundreds of years of custom, law, ceremony, ideas, and ideals about trans and genderqueer and non-binary lives. An artificial void, like there would be if you created the meanest black hole you can imagine – one that makes only that of which it disapproves of disappear completely.

In the shadow of that imposed and curated void, as trans people have been determinedly popping back up again in this crack and that crevice, and not being quite as vigorously plucked or squashed, cis people have a lot of questions. Like, why is this suddenly a thing? It's not, pumpkin.

A few threads and fragments of our history have escaped and survived – a few poems, some paintings, a couple of legal decisions – and we cherish them. They feel like reassurance, like validity – we have always been here; this has always been a thing. It may be that being a gender outlaw is still a radical act, but it is, as j wallace skelton writes, a radical act with a long history. But for a while, the suppression of our identities was so encompassing that we never even got enough light and air to sprout, never mind to grow and bloom. Now, like flowers reclaiming a meadow, we are popping out all over. Trans and genderqueer and non-binary are not remotely new things. That they – that we – are now visible in greater number than during any time in recorded history is just the natural order, reasserting itself.

In the time before gatekeeping, before the Harry Benjamin Standards, before medical intervention, before Piers Morgan shouting at people about their genitals on broadcast television, it was possible in many places to discuss one's gender with community members, elders, and friends. Professional intervention wasn't available, except to the degree that religious leaders might have been considered skilled workers and might have offered their advice, or even rulings, about the future roles and responsibilities available to a person.

What's most pleasing to me about the book you are currently holding – and there are many things about it that are very pleasing indeed – is that it feels like the beginning of a return. A return to the days in which our explorations of our own place in the lovely, spacious galaxies of gender were introspective and collaborative with others of our same experience, not performative and assessed with tick boxes. To be guided, tenderly, through questions and considerations of gender, to be not just allowed but encouraged to explore and play as a means of learning about one's own gender, feels like such a relief after the way things have been for such a while now.

Imagine if a person didn't feel as though they had to build and then justify their gender identity, if they could just experience it and then explain it.

I often wonder what's ahead for gender outlaws in the world – what the next ten years will bring (and sometimes what the next ten days will bring). I hope, always, for movement toward the destigmatizing, demedicalizing, and decolonizing of gender as a thing in the world. It's a relief to start seeing tools and matrices, concepts and frames, that put the power of our gender back with us – with people who are experiencing our own behaviors and desires. I appreciate and applaud all attempts to allow us, as j wallace skelton teaches, to be our own experts, and I am excited for you, dear reader, that perhaps you will never have to fill out a ream of forms and spend $20 you don't have a on a taxi to be sure you won't be late to an appointment you don't feel ready for. Well done to you for investing it in this book – and in yourself – instead. Read on.

Acknowledgements

This book could not have been written without the support of so many people, including our gender possibility models and queeros mentioned in Section 7 of this book. We are grateful first of all to the traditional custodians of the lands on which we have been raised, on which we currently live, and where we have written the book. We are particularly grateful to all the Indigenous elders and people who have helped gender-expansive lives to survive, thrive, and resist. We are thankful to all gender pioneers and ancestors, known and unknown, as well as to all the people who have written about this topic before us. Our work could not have happened without their work. We're thankful to Piers, Luisa, and Frith who hosted us in their beautiful haven (www.wild-retreats.com) to write this book, and to Catherine Forester, whose yoga course put us in the perfect mindset to do so (helixyoga.co.uk). Thank you to the Open University for providing additional funds to pay for Julia Scheele's work and to Julia Scheele for the wonderful images, including our book cover. We are thankful to all the people who we have worked with as therapists, supervisors, teachers, and co-organisers. Your stories were essential to the creation of this book. We're incredibly grateful to all the sensitivity readers, endorsers, and supporters. Thank you for your insight and enthusiasm. Any mistakes remain entirely our responsibility. Here are some specific acknowledgements from us both...

ALEX WRITES:

I could not do any of my work without the love and support of my spouse and co-parent, Michael Sinclair Wright, who has also been my companion on my gender adventures for nearly two decades. I am also grateful to my daughter, Melissa Iantaffi-Wright, for being the amazing person she is, every day; to my mom, Amelia Scalone, for giving me life, for being the best nonna ever to my child, and for being willing to keep growing with me; and to my sister, Miriam Iantaffi, for her brilliant writing. There are so many people who sustain me in so many ways that it is so hard to name them all. I am sorry if you are in my life and I forgot to thank you. I am grateful to you! Thank you to Danny Haag, my queer brother in dance, magic, and heart; to Copper Persephone for being an amazing housemate and cooking many meals; to Donald Engstrom-Reese for being one of my untameable siblings and teaching me so much; to Mark Engstrom-Reese for starting our queer family business with me; to Karin Levitski for her art and friendship; and to Eddy Samara, Chuck Leisinger, Max Gries, Cian McDonald, Diane Long, and Shor Salkas for being the siblings of my queer heart. I am so grateful to be in friendship and community with Billy Navarro Jr, Rox Anderson, and Andrea Jenkins, who continue to build, nurture, and mentor trans POC communities in the Twin Cities. Thank you to Susan Raffo for being a magnificent healer, mentor, and friend; to the People's Movement Center for nurturing my re-emergence as an independent practitioner; to Terri Bernard for being a wonderfully supportive therapist; to Blythe Davis for being a fabulous bodyworker and helping me take care of my body; to Barbara Nordstrom-Loeb for being an amazing friend, colleague, and dance and movement therapy teacher and mentor; to Bruce Minor for his incredible mentorship; to Markie Twist for her friendship and fierce encouragement; and to all my Somatic Experiencing teachers and colleagues. Thank you to Daz Saunders, for whom the term 'best friend' seems inadequate to capture our two decades of being in each other's lives. Thank you to Maria Oxland, John Hawkins, Chris Barron, and Ilaria Longo for being steadfast friends and always accepting me, no matter what my gender or sexuality. Finally, I would like to thank Meg-John Barker for being in my life in many ways over the years and for encouraging me to write again and again.

MEG-JOHN WRITES:

I would like to thank so many people who have helped me to come to the point of writing this book. I've mentioned some of them over the coming pages, but to them I would like to add my fab crew of H Howitt, Maz Michael, Meredith Reynolds, and Arian Bloodwood, who support so much of my experiencing in this area. Also the following: The Open Barbers – Greygory Vass and Felix Lane – for helping me to wrangle far more than just my haircut! Ben Vincent and Jos Twist for navigating our shifting relationships to the point that we can write together – yay! Jay Stewart and Gendered

Intelligence for their amazing work. Sophie Gamwell and Ed Lord for supporting more personal explorations. Jake Yearsley for being an utterly brilliant therapist. Alec Scott Rook, Sam Feeney, Juno Roche, Christine Burns, Ruth Pearce, Helen Belcher, Kat Gupta, Karen Pollock, Campbell X, Sabah Choudrey, Gavi Ansara, DK Green, Kris Black, LJ Potter, Alex Drummond, Lou Futcher, iggi moon, Folami Being, and so so many others for support and inspiration on- and off-line. Finally, I am deeply grateful to Alex Iantaffi for sticking with me all this time and for introducing me to so many important and valuable people and ideas that I'd never otherwise have had the confidence to write about.

INTRODUCTION

Hello and thank you for picking up this book. We hope you'll enjoy exploring gender with us over the coming pages. We're about to introduce you to the reasons why we wrote the book, who we are, and how you might want to use it. So make yourself comfortable as we're about to discuss many things that may feel personal, emotional, and potentially challenging in our journey. Don't worry, we'll be here for you throughout the book to remind you to go at your own pace and to use this book as a guide, not as some kind of measuring stick.

WHY THIS BOOK?

Gender has been much in the spotlight in recent years. For example, the cover of *Time* magazine in 2014 declared the 'transgender tipping point' in relation to a story about trans people of different ages.[1] This was in part the result of increased media representation, including several figures in the spotlight such as Chelsea Manning, Paris Lees,

---

1   Steinmetz, K. (2014) 'The transgender tipping point.' *Time*, 29 May.

Lana – and now also Lilly – Wachowski, Fox Fisher, Janet Mock, Rebecca Root, Laverne Cox, Bethany Black, Carmen Carrera, Chaz Bono, Caitlyn Jenner, Annie Wallace, Jack Monroe, and Andreja Pejić. We've also witnessed legal changes globally such as the recognition of a 'third gender' option on documents in India, Australia, and some other countries. We've had the 'Facebook gender revolution', where people can now identify according to over 50 different gender options and can also choose to use either 'she', 'he', or 'they' pronouns on their profiles.

A lot of the public attention has been on people whose gender seems to be outside of what might be considered the 'norm'. However, we're all participating in creating gender all the time. In this book we invite you to learn more about the broader history of gender as well as to deepen your understanding of your own gender – whatever that is. Given all the current attention, we thought this might be a good time to create a guide for people who want something of a map and compass in this vast and ever-changing gender landscape.

Let's consider why you may have decided to pick this book up or leaf through its digital content online.

WHO ARE YOU?

You might have taken a look at this book for many reasons. Maybe you're thinking about your own gender right now. Perhaps you're finding out about gender for the first time and some of what you're learning doesn't feel like a very good fit for you, or maybe you've always wanted to change something about your gender and you're worried it might be too late. Perhaps somebody close to you has talked to you about their gender and you're struggling to understand or want to respond in the best way possible. You may have come across genders you didn't know about through your job. You may have noticed people sharing their pronouns as well as their names during introductions in community meetings or educational settings. You may simply be aware of the news stories about gender that we mentioned earlier. Or somebody may have given you a copy of this book as a gift.

We really hope that this book will be readable for everyone, whatever your gender or existing knowledge in this area. One thing we've noticed is that often when we talk about gender we tend to think about other people. This book is an invitation to consider both your own *and* other people's genders, because – as we'll see – for many reasons we tend to be kinder to others when we know better where we're coming from ourselves.

Although this book is mainly written for a general audience, we believe that professionals can also benefit from engaging with it, especially if they haven't yet had the opportunity to do reflective work on their own gender. For example, your therapist, counsellor, youth worker, social worker, doctor, teacher, spiritual leader, or whoever will hopefully think about their own gender before talking with you about yours!

WHO ARE WE?

We're writing this book because we're both therapists, scholars, and community organisers who are trans-identified and work with people of all genders. We've noticed that while there are many wonderful books exploring personal biographies, or addressing gender in a more academic or activist way, there isn't a general guide to gender that we could recommend to anybody who wanted to find out more. We'll refer to existing books and resources that we've found useful at the end of every section, in case you want to explore things further. Basically, this is the book that we wish we'd had access to ourselves when we were younger!

Next we'll give you a brief introduction to who we are, and situate our own genders a bit. We come back several times over the course of the book to our own stories as examples, as well as drawing on those of other people we know, to get across the diversity of gender experience. We take confidentiality very seriously though, so the experiences we'll share with you in this book are not direct quotes from specific individuals. Rather they're a summary of the kind of things we've heard several times from different people over the years.

ALEX WRITES:

Hi! I'm a trans masculine person in my mid-40s. What that means is that people thought I was a girl when I was born, and that I identify as being somewhere in the masculine territory of gender. Don't worry if all these words don't make sense right now. We'll talk about language very soon after this Introduction. I'm Italian and I've spent many of my adult years first in the United Kingdom and then in the United States. I was born into a working-class family that valued education, and I was the first person in my family to pursue postgraduate education and to get a PhD. This was something that seemed very strange to my grandmother because of the sex assigned to me at birth! Growing up, I received some very specific messages about gender, which often didn't make sense to me. It took me quite a while to get to my current understanding of who I am, which is why I'm excited to share this book with you! As well as being a writer, scholar, therapist, and community organiser, I'm also a parent, spouse, and avid dancer. I use pronouns like 'he' or 'they'.

MEG-JOHN WRITES:

Hey! Gender-wise I'm a non-binary – or genderqueer – person in my early 40s. For me that means I feel somewhere in the middle of the spectrum between masculine and feminine, and that different sides of me are more 'masculine' or 'feminine' or 'androgynous'. As Alex says, we'll come back to all these words! Another interesting thing about me is that I grew up in a mixed-class family in the United Kingdom, and was surrounded at school by people from a lot of different cultures and faiths. So I had a lot of different gender models around me as a kid, but also ended up receiving a lot of pressure to be a certain kind of 'girl' if I wanted to find love and validation. I feel like my gender is an ongoing journey, linked to trying to become kinder towards myself. Embracing a non-binary gender in recent years has felt like a big part of that for me. I spend pretty much all my time writing, teaching, and doing therapy and community work. I also love comics and zines. I use 'they' pronouns – something we'll also come back to soon.

Something you might notice from these introductions is that we adopt an intersectional approach to gender. This means that we believe we all have many different aspects of our identities and experiences that relate to each other – or *intersect*. Some of these are more or less visible to others.

The term 'intersectionality' originated from a Black woman scholar, Kimberlé Crenshaw, who wanted to highlight how the experiences of Black women were different from those of Black men *and* White women because of the intersection of race and gender. Other authors, such as bell hooks and Patricia Hill Collins, have also talked about this. The idea of intersectionality has taken on a larger life in the past two decades and has been adopted by many people and stretched in various directions. In our book, the idea is key because gender is in a close relationship with all other aspects of our identities and experiences. If all of this sounds a little heady, we hope that it'll make more sense by the end of this book. We'll give plenty of practical examples to illustrate these more theoretical points.

HOW TO USE THIS BOOK

One important thing to say upfront is that in this book we're not saying that some ways of living our genders are better than others, or that anybody should compare themselves against other people's genders. However, it can sometimes be useful to see yourself reflected in somebody else who has a similar gender to your own. For this reason, we've included as many experiences and perspectives as we can. If we've left something out, feel free to let us know.

The book is divided into seven sections, and each section includes four main sub-sections. We start by exploring what gender is (Section 1). Then we move on to look at how the world around us understands gender (Section 2). After that we get personal and think more about your own gender background (Section 3). Then we encourage you to reflect on how you experience your gender today (Section 4).

Next we consider how you identify and live your gender at the moment, and what other possibilities there might be (Section 5). Following that, we think about your gender in relationships and in relation to your sexuality (Section 6). Finally we consider gender communities and role models you might like to draw on (Section 7).

There are activities and reflection points throughout the sections. These are opportunities for you to think about how what we've been saying relates to your own ideas and experiences. The activities tend to be slightly longer invitations to actually do something (e.g. draw a picture, remember something that happened to you, or talk with a friend). The reflection points are briefer pauses. You may want to write on this book itself, and/or use a notebook to keep track of your thoughts and responses to the activities as you go along. We recognise that people have different ways of learning, so we've given different options all the way through. You're also welcome to create your own! If you're reading this book as a group or a class, you can use the activities and reflection points as opportunities to share your journey with each other if that feels appropriate.

You don't need to work through the activities if you don't want to. It's fine just to read the book. If you're new to thinking about gender, you may want to start at the beginning and work your way through. If all this is more familiar territory for you, you may want to go to a specific section or sub-section, and that's fine. If you do that, but then find some of the terminology confusing, we invite you to return to Section 1, where we introduce many of the words and definitions used throughout the book. At the end of each section we've also signposted other available resources that might be helpful if you want to find out more about a specific topic.

Gender is a very personal subject and, in our experience, feelings often arise when talking about it. For example, some people feel deep sadness and loss about the periods of their lives when they could not express their gender in ways that felt comfortable for them. Others feel excitement and hope about the possibilities that are opening up at the moment, or about the things they're discovering about themselves and others through exploring their gender. Some feel fear, and even anger, about gender shifts in the world – and in the lives of people they know – because this is unfamiliar to them, because it makes them think uncomfortable thoughts about themselves, or because they believe it to be morally wrong.

We invite you to notice what comes up for you as you go through the book. Try to be curious about it, but also to hold it lightly, without judging yourself harshly for whatever you find yourself thinking, feeling, or experiencing. We encourage you to approach this topic with kindness towards yourself and others – including us, the authors. Our intention is definitely not to provide a rulebook, but rather to share with you what we've learned over many years through our personal and professional experiences; and of course there may be parts you disagree with or experience differently.

Triggers are words, experiences, stories, or places that evoke a strong emotional response because of our own individual, social, and cultural experiences. Gender is definitely a topic that can be triggering! Even though we haven't used trigger warnings in this book, we're aware that any part of the content might be a trigger for somebody somewhere. We encourage you to go slow, notice how you react to the material presented, stay kind to yourself, and don't hesitate to get support as needed.

To support you in engaging with this book kindly and openly, we've placed reminders throughout to slow down, breathe, notice your experience, take time out if you need to, and remain curious rather than judgemental, at least as much as you can. Sometimes these are just brief invitations to pause and breathe in the text, and sometimes there are full-page reminders with suggestions of something specific to do. Feel free to notice what works for you and what does not. These are just invitations, which we hope might be helpful.

Your first reminder is on the following page...

FURTHER RESOURCES

The following is a selection of books by writers mentioned in this Introduction:

- Collins, P.H. (2002) *Black Feminist Thought: Knowledge, Consciousness, and the Politics of Empowerment.* New York, NY: Routledge.

- Crenshaw, K. (1995) *Critical Race Theory: The Key Writings that Formed the Movement.* New York, NY: The New Press.

- hooks, b. (2000) *Feminist Theory: From Margin to Center.* London: Pluto Press.

Take a moment to notice where you are.

Do you feel comfortable, or at least neutral, in this place? If not, do you need to make any adjustments? Could you be a little more comfortable in this moment? What would you need to adjust to increase your comfort by 1 per cent right now? Maybe you want to shift the position you are in, breathe quietly for a few seconds, or take a sip of water.

Once you're settled in a comfortable place, take a moment to notice your surroundings.

If you notice something pleasing – maybe a colour, shape, sound, texture, or smell – take your time letting yourself have that experience of pleasure.

Take time to notice how your body makes contact with the furniture or ground, depending on where you are, and take some more time settling.

Breathe.

When you're ready, let's begin…

WHAT IS GENDER?

In this section we'll talk a bit about language, particularly defining some of the words that we're using through this book. Then we'll focus in on what the word 'gender' itself means and how it's different, or similar, to related words like 'sex' and 'sexuality'. After that we'll consider whether gender is something biological, psychological, or social (spoiler alert: it's a combination of all three!). And finally we'll explore some different dimensions of gender: How we identify our gender, what our gender roles are, how we express gender, and how we experience it.

1.1 WHAT WORDS MEAN

In recent years there's been an explosion of words around gender. For example, we mentioned in the Introduction how Facebook now offers its users over 50 different words to identify their gender on their profile, compared to the two words – 'male' or 'female' – that it used to offer.

All this new language can leave us feeling out of our depth and in dangerous waters. We can often feel very anxious about which words to use in case we get something wrong, especially if someone in our lives has asked us to use different language around their gender. It doesn't matter how familiar we are with these areas; even your authors occasionally get it wrong and have to apologise to somebody for having used the wrong name or pronoun.

Language changes fast as people and communities figure out what feels appropriate, so sometimes you find that a term or acronym that used to be the best one to use no longer is. Also, different terms can be more or less appropriate in different contexts. For example, for a while a lot of people in trans communities used 'trans*' with the idea that this was a more inclusive term, with the * standing in for various possible endings. But now most agree that 'trans' (without the *) is the more inclusive umbrella term. Also, different people prefer different versions of the LGBTQ (lesbian, gay, bisexual, trans, queer) acronym, with many adding extra Ts and Qs (for Two-Spirit and questioning) as well as A for asexual and I for intersex. Other people now use GSRD (gender, sexual, and relationship diversity) to move away from the ever-expanding alphabet soup. Where Alex lives, in the United States, the preferred term around race in many places is POC (for 'People of Colour'), or POCI (for 'People of Colour and Indigenous people'), whereas in the United Kingdom – where Meg-John lives – some use this and some prefer BAME (Black, Asian, and Minority Ethnic), while others consider the word 'Black' alone to be an important, encompassing, political term for the same communities. All of these terms may change again in the future because language is a living, breathing, relational phenomenon.

Often there isn't one 'right' terminology that you can learn, but rather it's about the following:

— Check with the group or person concerned – especially if you're not identified in the same way yourself – what their preferences are (this is sometimes called 'ask etiquette').

— Be prepared to practise as much as possible using the language they've asked you to use. Making sure that you use it all the time, including when they're not around as well as in their presence, is an important part of this.

— Apologise once if you get it wrong, and move on. Nobody wants you to dwell on your mistake.

— Keep checking in if you think that language use may have shifted over time.

The uncertainty raised by changing language can feel very threatening to some people. In our work we find that some respond to the defensiveness they feel by completely ignoring preferred terms and continuing to use the language they're comfortable with. For example, that might involve continuing to use 'she' pronouns for somebody who uses 'they'; or using the word 'transsexual' instead of 'trans' when asked what the T in LGBT is – many trans people dislike the term 'transsexual' because of its medical history, and because it doesn't include all trans people. Some folk go even further and argue that it's wrong for people to invent new language for their experiences, or to change the meaning of words over time.

Changing terminology

Let's address this last point. It's important to remember that words can and do change their meaning all of the time.

For example, in the area of gender, many words that were once horrible slurs have been reclaimed by the groups they targeted and are now being used in a positive way by those groups themselves. You can see this in the reclaiming of the word 'slut' by people in non-monogamous relationships – there's a key book in this community called *The Ethical Slut* (see Further Resources for details) – or by the feminists who marched in the slut walks to challenge damaging myths around rape and sexual violence. Similarly, the word 'queer' used to be an insult, and now many LGBT+ people, and others, use it proudly to describe themselves.

On the other hand, some words that used to be deemed acceptable in the past now certainly aren't. For example, we tend to use 'gay' rather than 'homosexual', and 'intersex' rather than 'hermaphrodite' because, as with 'transsexual', the latter words were used in the past to suggest that those groups had some kind of abnormality or disorder. Sadly, some words are erased completely when groups are colonised or eradicated. For example, the term 'Two-Spirit' is an English-based word created by a coalition of diverse Indigenous people to indicate numerous gender and sexual identities and roles that existed in the languages of several tribal nations across the globe but were lost through genocide and colonisation.

New words are also invented or adapted all the time to capture or enable experiences that we didn't have language for previously. For example, we'll see at the end of Sub-section 1.1 that non-binary people have developed many words to describe the diversity of experiences they have. The singular use of the pronoun 'they' dates back as far as the works of Chaucer and Shakespeare, and for centuries people have used it when they don't know the gender of a person, as in: 'Somebody's left their bag behind. I hope they realise before they get too far.' However, it's only fairly recently that this singular use of 'they' has been embraced by non-binary and genderqueer communities. For example: 'Meg-John is one of the authors of this book. They use "they" pronouns because their experience is that they're somewhere between or beyond the binary of male and female.'

It's important, therefore, to remember that words are always being invented in all kinds of contexts: that's how language develops. It's also vital to be mindful that words have different resonances in different times and places, which makes it even more important to check in with any person or community that you're in contact with. For example, elders who remember being called 'queer' as an insult often feel much less comfortable describing themselves in that way, and some trans people still do like to use the word 'transsexual' for themselves.

Reflection point: The words you use

Think about the words that you, and others, currently use to describe or indicate your gender. These could be words like 'Madam', 'Sir', 'man', 'woman', 'girl', 'lady', 'gentleman', 'chap', 'trans', 'queer', and so on. Maybe make a note of the ones you prefer, and any that don't feel so comfortable to you.

Are there any words around gender that you've heard used that you don't completely understand? Make a note of these too. Hopefully we'll be coming back to most of them, but feel free to also have an online search if you have internet access.

The importance of language

Our language around gender is very important for many reasons. Here are just a few of them:

 — Language often shapes our experience more than we realise. For example, when the generic 'man' is used to mean human, as in 'mankind' or 'every man for himself', people who are not men often don't remember what has been said as well, and experience lower confidence afterwards than when inclusive language like 'human' or 'person' is used. This can become a barrier to learning in education, or wellbeing in healthcare. Researchers have also found that we learn, through language and images, to treat men as the 'norm' and compare women to them – for example, in the way that graphs and tables tend to present data from men before data from women, or how we generally phrase explanations of any gender differences in terms of how women are different from men (e.g. 'women are more persuadable than men', rather than 'men are more stubborn than women'). For this reason we've tried to mix up our ordering throughout this book when talking about women and men, instead of going for the standard order of 'male and female', 'boys and girls', or 'husband and wife'. Of course such phrases also imply that gender is binary – we'll come back to that in a moment.

 — Language enables different – often more positive – experiences. For example, for many trans and/or non-binary people, finding that there is a word that feels like a good fit for them is part of what enables them to express themselves in ways that feel congruent and comfortable, as well as helping them to explain their experience to others. Having a shared language for something can make it feel more legitimate, and understandable.

– Language can be used to include or to exclude people, to respect or to reject them. For example, sometimes it can feel very valuable for a marginalised group to have an 'X-only' space (e.g. bisexual-only, or people-of-colour-only) where they can talk about some of their experiences in relative safety with people who share these experiences. On the other hand, exclusive policies can easily divide and fragment communities, such as women's events that don't welcome trans women often using problematic language to define who 'counts' as a woman. We'll come back to these kinds of complexities in Section 7.

ACTIVITY: ALL OF THE WORDS

Below are all the words that Facebook was offering for gender when we were writing this book. You might find it useful to circle any words that feel like a good fit for you (there may well be more than one of them), and also to reflect on any that other people might use for you that you don't like, and any that are unfamiliar to you. You could also notice whether any of the words you know or like are missing. For example, we notice that it doesn't include words like 'lady', 'girl', 'tomboy', 'butch', or 'femme'.

Asexual, Agender, Androgyne, Androgynes, Androgynous, Bigender, Cis, Cis Female, Cis Male, Cis Man, Cis Woman, Cisgender, Cisgender Female, Cisgender Male, Cisgender Man, Cisgender Woman, Female to Male, Female to Male Trans Man, Female to Male Transgender Man, Female to Male Transsexual Man, F2M, FTM, Gender Fluid, Gender Neutral, Gender Nonconforming, Gender Questioning, Gender Variant, Genderqueer, Hermaphrodite, Intersex, Intersex Man, Intersex Person, Intersex Woman, Male to Female, Male to Female Trans Woman, Male to Female Transgender Woman, Male to female transsexual woman, Man, M2F, MTF, Neither, Neutrois, Non-binary, Other, Pangender, Polygender, T* man, T* woman, Trans, Trans Female, Trans Male, Trans Man, Trans Woman, Trans Person, Trans*Female, Trans*Male, Trans*Man, Trans*Person, Trans*Woman, Transsexual, Transsexual Female, Transsexual Male, Transsexual Man, Transsexual Person, Transsexual Woman, Transgender Female, Transgender Person, Transmasculine, Two* Person, Two-Spirit, Two-Spirit Person, Woman.

Remember that this list developed in a particular time and place, which means that many more possible words are also missing. We'll come back to this point in Section 2.

FIGURE 1.1: GENDER OPTIONS

We'll give you a brief overview here of the meaning of a few key terms. We'll explain all of these, and more, in further detail as you go through the rest of the book.

— *Intersex*, or *diversity of sex development (DSD)*, refers to people who are born with reproductive, chromosomal and/or sexual anatomy that doesn't seem to fit the typical definitions of female or male. In other words, people who were present at the person's birth – or often later in their life – had some uncertainty about which sex to assign them, or determined that neither of the available binary options was suitable for their biological make-up.

— *Trans* (or *transgender*) refers to people who no longer identify with the sex they were assigned at birth. *Cis* (or *cisgender*) refers to people whose sex assigned at birth and gender identity are 'on the same side', which is literally the meaning of the Latin prefix 'cis' (the prefix 'trans', also from Latin, means 'across'). We might talk about *trans women* and *trans men*, and *cis women* and *cis men*, although it's not usually polite to include somebody's trans or cis status in their description unless it's directly relevant to what you're saying and you're sure that the person is happy with you doing so. For example, revealing somebody's trans status who doesn't want it revealed is illegal in the United Kingdom and many other countries. Most non-binary or genderqueer people are trans in that they haven't remained in the sex they were assigned at birth, given that very few people are assigned non-binary. However, not all genderqueer or non-binary people feel comfortable referring to themselves as trans, so it's always worth checking and asking directly how people identify.

— *Non-binary, genderqueer, NB,* or *enby* are umbrella terms for people who fall outside the male/female binary. There are lots of different experiences – with different words – under this umbrella. For example: *agender* and *gender-neutral* people have no gender; *androgyny* often refers to being somewhere between masculinity and femininity – or mixing together elements of both; *demi-boys* and *demi-girls* feel only to some extent a boy or a girl; *third-gender* people experience themselves as a further gender beyond male and female; *bigender* and *genderfluid* people move between genders over time; *pangender* people may have multiple or plural gender experiences;

genderfuck people more deliberately – often politically – try to challenge the binary gender system, as do some who prefer the term *genderqueer*. Some NB people use the words *butch* or *femme* to refer to the sense that they see themselves in a particularly masculine or feminine way, while recognising that this is part of a non-binary gender system.

– *Drag* refers to deliberately performing a version of gender that is often hyper-masculine or -feminine; for example, drag kings and drag queens do this. Although drag is often associated with somebody performing the 'opposite' role to their sex assigned at birth, actually anybody can do drag, regardless of their sex/gender.

That'll do for definitions for now! Onto the word 'gender' itself...

1.2 SEX/GENDER AND GENDER/SEXUALITY

Now that we've explored what's happening with language, and why language is important, let's take a more in-depth look at some of the key words used frequently in this book: 'sex', 'gender', and 'sexuality'. These words are used in everyday contexts, so you may feel that you already have a pretty good understanding of what they mean. But maybe it's not so simple. For example, when we talk about gender, what are we really talking about? While we'll address the different components of gender in Sub-section 1.3, we want to take a few moments here to define some differences, as well as highlighting the relationships between sex, gender, and sexuality.

What is sex?

Sex is often assigned at birth by medical professionals and parents, usually on the basis of the genitals a baby happens to be born with. If someone is born with a penis, they're generally assigned male; if someone is born with a vagina, they're generally assigned female; and if their genitals are deemed to be ambiguous, they might be assigned intersex. A person might be assigned as intersex later in life as well, if they discover that their chromosomal make-up doesn't match what people had assumed based on their genitals at birth. The reason we're using the word 'assigned' is because sex is more complicated than genital appearance. In fact, sex is a set of attributes, including – but not limited to – genitals. For example, sex also includes our chromosomal make-up. Very few of us know whether our chromosomal make-up matches our sex assigned at birth! Sex also includes other attributes, usually regulated by hormones, called 'secondary characteristics', such as chest growth/appearance, facial and body hair, voice, muscle mass, and fat distribution, to name but a few.

When talking about sex, we usually think of a binary biological division between male and female. However, the ways in which our bodies are structured externally and internally are not inherently male or female. For example, penises and vaginas are not inherently male or female. As mentioned in the previous paragraph, when conflating sex with genitals, we also ignore a large portion of our inner anatomy, that is, our chromosomal make-up. It is very difficult to know what sex we really are unless we take into consideration each possible facet of our internal as well as external structures. If you think this is all getting a little too complicated, let's consider the fact that sex itself is also not binary in nature. There are several variations and combinations of inner and outer characteristics in plants, animals, and humans. Those variations include plants and animals that even change their sex characteristics over time based on, and in response to, environmental conditions. As George Michael sang in the 1980s, sex might be natural, and even good, but it sure is not as easy as those pink and blue bows might lead us to believe!

From sex to gender

One of the challenges here is that the word 'sex' is used in a most confusing way in the English language, as well as in some other languages. Sex might refer to how someone has been assigned at birth, which then often leads people to assume rather a lot about a child's future gender identity, expressions, and roles. In this way, sex and gender are often used interchangeably, even though they are quite different concepts. 'Sex' might also be used to refer to sexual behaviours, confusing matters even more! One common example of sex and gender being used as synonyms is the phrase 'same-sex marriage' to indicate the union between people of the same gender. If sex and gender are two different concepts, what is gender?

While sex is based on a complex set of inner and outer physical characteristics, gender is a broad term that might indicate our identity, expressions, roles, or even larger sets of sociocultural expectations. Most humans develop a sense of their own gender identity in the early years of their childhood, but this can also change over time. This identity may match, or be different from, their gender expressions and roles, as we explain later in this book.

Although the distinction between sex and gender is often made as sex being about physical attributes, and gender being about social expectations, you'll see that matters are much more complicated than this. For example, just like with sex, people often think of gender as being binary: male or female. In the same way that nature has much more variation than we might initially think, so gender is far less flat and much more multifaceted. Sub-section 1.3 on gender being biopsychosocial will explore this in more detail. So let's now shift our attention to sexuality.

What is sexuality?

Sexuality is a complex web of desires, attractions, behaviours, and identities. The word is used to describe another really challenging concept that includes many aspects of who we are. People often think of sexuality as being straight or gay, that is, being attracted to people of the same gender or the opposite gender. However, as with sex and gender, things are a little more complicated. One aspect of sexuality is certainly about who we might be attracted to. However, even our attraction can be broken down into different aspects, such as physical, romantic, sexual, emotional, and even spiritual. We might find some people very physically attractive, but other people might turn us on sexually, whereas others still are those we feel closest to emotionally or spiritually.

Sexual attractions and behaviours are also more complex than straight or gay, as many people are attracted to, and/or engage sexually with, people of more than one gender. Such people might identify in a range of ways, including bisexual, pansexual, fluid, or even straight. Sexual identities are, in fact, similarly complex, and they are not always in line with our attractions or behaviours. For example, a person might identify as straight, which for them might mean being attracted to women. The same person might be physically attracted to, and engage in sexual behaviours with, men and genderqueer people.

Some aspects of our sexuality are not at all related to our own or other people's genders. For example, someone might experience little to no sexual attraction. Others might be turned on by specific scenarios, materials, or sensations. You can look forward to reading and learning a lot more about sexuality in Section 6.

Gender, sex, and sexuality are, as you can see, three different concepts. Each one is fairly complex and includes several aspects of who we are, weaving multifaceted portraits that usually change over time, as we grow and develop. Despite being separate, gender, sex, and sexuality are also in a relationship with each other. Our sex is in many ways part of our understanding of gender, and our sexuality is often, but not always, in a relationship to our own and other people's genders. Sexuality can also be in a relationship with sex, both our own and other people's, including, for some people, choices around reproduction.

These three terms can be thought of as members of a family. In a family the parents, siblings, cousins, aunts and uncles, grandparents, and so on might well be related, but they also have distinct roles and characteristics. Similarly, sex, gender, and sexuality have significant relationships with each other, while remaining distinct in their domains.

Below are some examples from a range of people we've interacted with over the years. As explained in the Introduction, none of these are quotes from a specific individual, but rather examples of the kinds of experiences we've heard over time from many people.

Multiple experiences: Sex, gender, and sexuality

'I just couldn't figure it out. I was born female, I am attracted to men, but I never felt comfortable wearing skirts, make-up, or spending time with girls, like I felt I was supposed to do. People kept assuming I was a lesbian, and even I wondered about it for some time. Eventually I realised that's just who I was. I am a masculine woman, attracted to men.'

'People kept wanting me to choose, but I just couldn't. I've always been sexually attracted to women and femininity, while feeling much more relaxed with and emotionally close to masculine people, regardless of their gender. I now identify as a bisexual, homoromantic trans man.'

'Everyone assumes I'm gay because they think I'm "soft" and "artistic" for a man. I guess my mannerisms can be more effeminate than those of most guys. However, I am straight through and through. I just can't be bothered with proving my masculinity in a way other people want me to.'

'I love everything about femininity: the clothes, make-up, the fierce feminist history. I am just a proud femme who also happens to be a lesbian. Unfortunately, often people assume I'm straight, even at lesbian events. They also seem surprised at my job as a mechanical engineer. I always liked pulling things apart, figuring out how they work, and putting them back together, or even making them better!'

'I've never felt at home in dresses or lipsticks. I always wanted to play with boys. Eventually I found other people like me and who were into me. I am a stud and proud of who I am.'

Reflection point: Who are you?

Now that we've defined the terms 'gender', 'sex', and 'sexuality' a bit more, how would you describe your own sex, gender, and sexuality? You can write about it here or use a notebook if you prefer.

Sex _____

Gender _____

Sexuality _____

1.3 GENDER IS BIOPSYCHOSOCIAL

People are often very concerned with questions of whether gender is something that's determined for us by our brains or hormones; whether it's something that we develop over time because of the social messages and rules we're exposed to; or whether perhaps it's something that we can choose for ourselves.

From science to the media to everyday conversations, these kinds of nature/nurture debates run deep, often with the assumption that one side of that divide is somehow more correct than the other. For example, think about common questions that are raised about whether trans people are 'really' the gender that they say they are – with 'really' often being a stand-in for issues of biology. This is because, at the moment, in Anglo-American culture things are often seen as more legitimate if they can be shown to have a 'cause' in our brains or our DNA.

We'd like to emphasise here that it really shouldn't matter whether a person's gender is biological, psychological, or social, or some combination of the three. It also shouldn't matter whether it's a choice or something that we 'can't help'. A person's experience is their experience, and the many and complex reasons behind it – even if we could figure them all out – shouldn't make a difference to whether we treat a person well or not, recognise their human rights, or try to help them be as comfortable and fulfilled as possible in the world.

However, given that people are often concerned with such questions, let's give them a moment. Our best evidence in this area comes from anthropology. Studies have found that people with diverse and expansive gender experiences and expressions have existed over time and space: taking different forms through all historical periods and across various cultures all over the globe. We'll come back to this in more detail in Section 2. For now it's just important to remember that gender diversity is nothing new. The Internet did not invent it!

The big word: 'Biopsychosocial'

We like the word 'biopsychosocial' to capture the fact that, for all of us, gender experience is a complex mix of our biology, our psychology, and the social world around us. We know that we're using the word 'complex' a lot here, but it really reflects reality! It's also kind of beautiful. Given that everybody's biological make-up, psychological experiences, and social context connect up in unique and complex ways, our gender really is something like a snowflake: no two of us are quite the same. Yet, just like we can recognise what a snowflake is, we can still find people who share some aspects of their gender identities and experiences with us.

Also the biological, the psychological, and the social: all feed back into each other in – you guessed it – complex ways. It might seem obvious, for example, that somebody's biology can impact their psychological experiences. For example, if somebody has a largely 'female' body and brain, that might mean that they are potentially more physically able to do certain things rather than others; perhaps even that they are more drawn to certain activities. But have you considered that our psychological experiences also impact *back* on our body and brain? If a kid is encouraged into rough and tumble play and sports from a very young age, they're likely to develop a very different physique to those kids who are not encouraged into similar activities. And we know from neuroscience that kids' brains develop differently depending on what activities they're encouraged into. When we learn to cook, or to kick a ball, the learning imprints itself onto our brains so that we're able to remember how to do it, and to do it better over time. Importantly, when it comes to gender, kids learn pretty quickly which things they're meant to be interested in and which they're not, and this can easily shape a good deal of their lives: the skills they learn, and the opportunities that are therefore available to them or not. When we repeat gender behaviours again and again and again in our everyday lives, like the pitch of our voice, the way that we walk, or how we respond to various situations, that way of doing things becomes imprinted on our bodies and brains. No wonder it ends up feeling 'natural' – there is so much reinforcement that happens all around us!

Of course that is where the social comes in. The cultural messages we receive about what is appropriate for somebody of our gender shape which things we do and don't do.

They also shape which things we find pleasurable because we get a lot of rewards and approval for doing them, whereas we may be shamed and punished for doing activities that do not meet other people's approval. All of this maps itself onto our developing bodies and brains. But, of course, our experiences can shape society too. Each wave of feminism has shifted the cultural messages that people receive about gender in important ways, and the current explosion of gender is also shifting things. So each generation has different options available to it, and may therefore experience its genders in different ways too.

Perhaps the easiest method of getting across the ways in which gender is biopsychosocial is by providing a few people's own understandings of how their genders came to be the way that they are.

Multiple experiences: Biopsychosocial gender

'My mum said I was really outgoing from the word "go", always wanting to go further and faster than everyone else. Maybe I was wired that way. Anyway, that was definitely not how girls were supposed to act in the place I grew up. I ended up making a big fuss and being the first girl there to join the Scouts. Now I definitely think of myself as a tomboy, and as a feminist. I'm a mum myself and I'm making sure that my girls have all of the options available to them.'

'I definitely had that thing of knowing I'd been assigned the wrong sex. Not all trans people have it, I know, but I did. I just knew that I was a girl. I was lucky my parents were pretty clued up about such things. They let me wear dresses at home, and they got somebody in to talk to my school. I went on puberty blockers at 12 years, and now

I take hormone replacements. I am what I've always been: a woman.'

'For me, growing up was pretty gender neutral. I liked "boys' toys" and "girls' toys" equally. But at school it was like you had to pick a side. And everybody saw me as a girl. I tried really hard to become proper feminine, but it always felt fake, you know? I eventually stopped trying. I was so happy when I found out about bigender in my thirties. Finally I had a word that fit me.'

'Most of my life, things were simple. I was a man's man: I did sports, worked on a building site, drank down the pub. Then I got prostate cancer in my fifties. What a lot of people don't know is that it often affects your sex drive radically. And the treatment can make you more emotional and "feminise" your body a bit too. Surprisingly for me, once I stopped fighting it, my wife and I both realised that we liked the changes. It seemed to make me a little softer and kinder. At least after I stopped feeling angry about it! The guys down the pub took a bit longer to come round, but now I notice that they're changing too. Going through this with me has helped them to open up and talk about their problems more.'

Reflection point: Gender shifts

After reading through these examples, think about how your own gender might shift – or stay the same – across different social situations and relationships. For example, do you notice that you change how you express your gender with different people or in different contexts, such as at work and at home, in public and in private? Perhaps you wear somewhat different clothes, or your tone of voice changes, for example.

FIGURE 1.2: MULTIPLE GENDER EXPRESSIONS

Opening up and closing down gender possibilities

You can see from the different experiences described above, that while a lot of us start out open to various possible expressions and experiences, our gender is often policed very early on, and generally in a binary way. This prevents us from exploring all of the different options, which is an important part of gender development. Many people are never allowed to try all of the different available toys and games, or to wear whatever clothes they fancy. Instead they're forced down the blue or pink aisle, and into the boys' or girls' clothing department. A lot of us end up having to undo the work that those messages have done to us, experimenting later in life with other options because we didn't have the opportunity as a kid. We'll think more about the impact that this restriction of options can have on people of all genders in Section 2.

To sum up Sub-sections 1.2 and 1.3, gender is diverse rather than binary at every level: biological, psychological, and social. Here are a few points:

- *Biological:* There is diversity in our chromosomal make-up, our levels of circulating hormones, the size and shape of our genitals, our secondary sex characteristics like hairiness or chest size, our physiques, and our brain structures and chemistry. None of these things can be divided into simply 'male' and 'female' boxes. A lot of people are somewhere between the two extremes on a spectrum, and some fit better in the 'opposite' box than the one that might be expected from their assigned sex at birth. Biologically, there are also far more and bigger differences between individual people than there are between large groups of people such as 'men' and 'women'.

- *Psychological:* There's also diversity in every aspect of our psychology, such as our ability at different subjects, our character, our values, and so on. There are far more similarities between the genders in most of these things than there are differences, and few people fit the expected boxes in every way.

- *Social:* There have been times and places where everyone has acted in the way we currently think of as 'masculine', and where everyone has acted in the way we currently think of as 'feminine'. There have also been examples where the roles are the opposite of what they are in dominant Anglo-American culture

– for example, women being more aggressive and violent, and men being more nurturing and social. As we'll see in Section 2, in many times and places, people have believed that there were more than two genders.

Also, as we've seen, all three of these aspects of our biopsychosocial gender experience interact and interconnect in complex and unique ways.

Finally, all of these things alone – and in combination – change over time. Our bodies and brains develop and age; we have different experiences that shape memory, personality, attitudes, and so on; and the world around us changes, giving us different messages about what's appropriate – or not – for people of our gender. We'll say a lot more about how our gender shifts over time – or is *fluid* – in Section 3.

1.4 MULTIPLE DIMENSIONS: IDENTITIES, ROLES, EXPRESSIONS, EXPERIENCES

We mentioned earlier that gender is multifaceted. As well as being a term that describes expectations in a specific culture, place, and point in time, it also refers to aspects of our identities, roles, expressions, and experiences. Let's start with some definitions of those terms, since we're still in Section 1 and getting oriented to this whole idea of gender.

Defining different aspects of gender: Identity

When talking about gender, it's important to break it down, given that it covers so many aspects of who we are, the expectations we might have of ourselves and others, and what we might experience as a consequence of these expectations, both at individual and collective levels. Gender identity is usually defined as an inner sense of who we are. However, this inner sense of our identity does not exist in isolation from the world around us. Our inner sense of self is influenced by many aspects of our lives. For example, it's shaped by language, family of origin, culture, place, race, ethnicity, historical moment, socioeconomic status, class, embodied experiences, and by how others react to and interact with us.

Some examples of words that describe gender identity are: 'man', 'woman', 'non-binary', 'Two-Spirit', 'trans man', 'trans woman', 'stud', 'genderqueer', 'man of transgender history', 'woman of transgender history', 'aggressive', 'gender fluid', and so on. You may remember some of those words from earlier parts of Section 1.

Children start to have a sense of their own gender identity in the early years, as they first differentiate between themselves and their caregivers, and then progressively between themselves and the rest of the world. It's at this point that children start to have a sense of their gender identity, as they notice physical, behavioural, and other differences between themselves and their peers, and in-between people generally. Children can also be acutely aware, usually more than most adults think, of what's safe to express and what isn't, by the time they are three or four years old. We'll discuss this further later in the book, especially in Sections 2 and 3.

Gender identity is a sense of who we are, in relation to this broader idea of gender in the world we've come into. Do we fit with what others reflect back to us, or do we not? How do we fit or not fit? This process happens so early on that, for many people, it can feel almost as if it's unconscious. This might be particularly true if you've always felt at home with the expectations that other people have had of you because of your sex assigned at birth. Sometimes people refer to this as 'cis privilege'. This means that because your sex assigned at birth is aligned with your gender identity (which is often what people expect in most dominant cultures in the United Kingdom, United States, and many other places), you may never have needed to think about gender very much, and it all felt very 'natural' to you, gender-wise. However, some trans people also feel that their gender identity emerged easily, and clearly, while some cis people really struggled with gender expectations growing up. There is simply not one way of experiencing things when it comes to gender, and no easy generalisations that can be made.

Reflection point: Your gender identity

Take a moment to breathe and to think about your early years, as far back as you can go. Don't worry if it's not too far at all – that's OK. Can you remember one of the first times that you realised what your gender was? It's OK if you can't. It can be as simple as being divided into girls and boys in school to line up, or for an activity, and having an inner sense of where you belonged. That inner sense may or may not have matched what others expected of you. Take a breath and notice what sensations, thoughts, and emotions emerge as you let yourself spend some time with those memories, if that feels tolerable. If it doesn't, shake it off, and do something to find some sense of wellbeing, or neutrality, before coming back to the rest of the book.

Defining different aspects of gender: Expression

Gender expression is usually how your inner sense of self (your identity) is expressed outwardly. Gender expression refers to the ways we talk and move, the clothes and shoes we wear, how we do our hair, and how we might manifest this sense of self through make-up, accessories, and how we interact with others and the environment around us. The way we interact with others starts to flow into the territory of gender roles, so we'll come back to this in a moment.

People around us might often make assumptions about our gender identity based on our gender expression, even though these may or may not match up. Such assumptions are usually based on stereotypes, and therefore on a very limited range of gender expressions. We'll discuss gender stereotypes in more detail in Section 2. For now, we want to make sure you know that there can be many gender expressions, just like there are many gender identities. Some words used to describe gender expressions are: 'androgynous', 'feminine', 'masculine', 'butch', 'femme', 'fluid', and so on. Some of those words can also be identities, which is where it gets a bit confusing again. There's no way to tell if a certain word indicates an identity or an expression for someone unless you ask them. For example, some people have a strong identity as femme, whereas someone might identify as a trans man, a genderqueer person, or a cis woman, and see femme as an expression of their gender, but not necessarily as part of their identity.

In the same way in which our identity is shaped by our language, culture, family of origin, race, ethnicity, spirituality, class, embodied experiences, and so on, our gender expressions also don't operate in isolation. They're shaped by, and intersect with, our gender identity and other aspects of our identities and experiences. We'll explore those intersections more fully in Section 3.

Sometimes gender expression is also referred to as 'presentation'. In this book we've favoured the use of the term 'gender expression', as we find it to be broader and more inclusive than 'presentation'. If we want to complicate things a little bit more, we could also mention that gender presentation can sometimes be more of a combination of gender expression and role, that is, how we present ourselves, gender-wise, to the wider world.

Defining different aspects of gender: Role

Gender role is about the way we enact our gender in specific environments and in relation to other people. Our gender role might be fairly fixed across different spaces and social situations, or it might be more changeable, according to where we are and who we're with. Words that describe gender roles can be similar to those that describe gender expressions. However, gender identity, expression, and role can all be different to one another. For example, a person can identify as a woman, have an androgynous expression, and a masculine gender role in most domains of her life. If you're feeling confused right now, hang in there: it will all become clearer as you read the book!

Gender roles are tricky, because they're often so specific to each culture and point in time. For example, some people might think of a feminine role as being nurturing, yielding, accommodating, and passive, whereas others might think of the same role as powerful, protective, active, and strong.

We might feel more or less safe expressing our gender roles authentically in different places, or with different people.

We might also genuinely experience more comfort with one gender role in one area of our life, and a different gender role in another. Many people tend to interact differently, gender-wise, in different environments, with different people, and also at different times in their lives, or even according to what time of the day it is, and how they might be feeling! Other people might have more fixed gender roles. Once again, there's no right or wrong way of doing gender.

Defining different aspects of gender: Experience

Gender experience is the impact and manifestation of a range of intersections in our lives. It's about how we're perceived and how we perceive others; how we might be able to move safely in the world, or not, because of who we are. It touches every aspect of our lives, from how much we get paid, to who we can marry. It impacts everything, from whether we can walk somewhere without fear of violence, to where we can worship or socialise.

Gender experiences vary across time and space, and while we often feel their impact individually, they can be shared across groups of people who have common identities, expressions, or roles. For example, some young women might share the experience of being cat-called in the street; some professional men might share the experience of being called 'Sir' in shops and restaurants; some non-binary people might share the experience of being faced with only binary bathroom options in public places.

Gender experiences can further validate or invalidate our sense of who we are, how we express ourselves, and the roles we play in the world. They are closely interlinked to other aspects of our identities mentioned earlier, such as race, ethnicity, class, disability, sexuality, and so on. We might share some aspects of our gender experiences with certain people, and some with others. For example, Black women, as a larger category, share specific gender experiences that are quite different from those of White women in the United States and the United Kingdom. However, a middle-class Black woman might have some shared experiences of gender around class with other middle-class women. She might also feel that some of her gender experiences are different from those of working-class Black women, while still having many shared experiences with them around being Black and a woman. Gender experiences are varied, just like identities, expressions, and roles, and intersect with every aspect of who we are!

ACTIVITY: GENDER IDENTITIES, ROLES, EXPRESSIONS, AND EXPERIENCES

We're going to build up a little from the Reflection Point in Sub-section 1.3. Take a moment to consider different environments and situations, and to make notes about how your gender identities, expressions, roles, and experiences may change or stay the same. If they change, what is it that shifts and why? Here's a table to get you started. However, please feel free to make up your own table, or complete this activity in any way that you prefer (e.g. journaling, drawing, writing poetry, expressing this through music, exploring through dance, or making a mind map).

Situation	Identities	Expressions	Roles	Experiences
Work				
Family of origin				
Friends				
Chosen family				
Faith community				
Club/group				
At home				
With strangers				
On vacation				

Reflection point: Gender and those around you

Think about people around you. Have you ever talked to them about their gender identities, expressions, roles, and experiences? Have you made assumptions about their gender identities, roles, and experiences based on their expression? What would it be like to have a conversation with a person of your choice – someone you trust to do this with – about your own and their gender identities, expressions, roles, and experiences?

> **REMEMBER:** Gender is a vast and wonderful landscape. However, we're often not brought up to realise just how vast this landscape is, and how many possibilities there are. If someone else's experiences are different from yours and don't seem to make sense to you, take a moment to breathe. In the same way that the Northern Lights are no less real or beautiful just because they are rare and unseen by many, all gender identities, expressions, roles, and experiences can exist, co-exist, and enrich our collective gender landscape.

FURTHER RESOURCES

You can read about relationship possibilities in:

— Hardy, J.S. and Easton, D. (2017) *The Ethical Slut: A Practical Guide to Polyamory, Open Relationships, and Other Freedoms in Sex and Love.* Berkeley, CA: Ten Speed Press.

You can read more about gender and language in this book:

— Cameron, D. (2007) *The Myth of Mars and Venus.* Oxford: Oxford University Press.

The following website is a good place to find out the meaning of various gender words:

— www.gender.wikia.com

You can read more about the neuroscience of gender and how it's biopsychosocial in this book:

— Fine, C. (2010) *Delusions of Gender: How Our Minds, Society, and Neurosexism Create Difference.* New York, NY: WW Norton & Company.

This book is a really good one for explaining diversity across biology, psychology, and social understandings of gender:

- Fausto-Sterling, A. (2012) *Sex/Gender: Biology in a Social World*. London: Routledge.

Take a breath.

What do you notice in this moment?

Can you feel the contact between your
body, and the surface you are sitting or lying
on? What do you sense around you?

Keep breathing.

Talking about gender might activate
all sorts of sensations, emotions,
and reactions in us. That's OK.

If you find yourself feeling floaty, wound up, or
losing interest, it's OK to take a break. In fact, we
actively encourage you to take as many breaks
as you need and want while reading this book!

You could write down your thoughts and feelings,
talk to a trusted friend, draw or paint, or just
move your body to reconnect with yourself,
and always come back to your breath.

When you're ready, come back for Section 2…

HOW THE WORLD SEES GENDER

In Section 1 we discussed how gender can be about who we are, how we interact with ourselves and the world, and what expectations we have for ourselves and each other. Now we turn our attention to the broader context. In this section we explore where ideas of gender come from, whether those ideas are universal or not (spoiler alert: they aren't!), what generalisations people make about gender, how those stereotypes can impact us, and finally what some of the current options around gender are in the contexts in which we live.

Please remember that all of the ideas presented here, and in the rest of the book, are not the definitive truth across the globe. While we try to consider diverse and global perspectives, we ourselves are based in specific geographical, cultural contexts, that is, the United Kingdom and the United States, and things might be different where you live. We encourage you to do your own research, especially for issues highlighted in Sub-section 2.4.

One more word of caution, before we begin: if all this still feels a little more theoretical than you wanted or expected, don't worry – we're going to get much more personal in Section 3. But because gender is so influenced by our wider culture, it seems important to start there.

2.1 GENDER ACROSS TIME AND SPACE

We mentioned earlier that some of the best evidence we have about the existence of gender diversity across time and space comes from anthropology and history. We also made the bold statement that the Internet did not create gender diversity! We'll present some evidence to back up these claims in a moment. Before we do that, let's have a look at what gender looks like in the societies where we, as authors, are currently located.

A short ramble around gender in dominant cultures

While both of us are often surrounded by a broad range of gender identities, expressions, roles, and experiences in our everyday lives, we're also aware that there is a potentially less diverse landscape when it comes to the dominant cultures in which we live. By dominant cultures, we mean those that shape our everyday language and thinking through all sorts of widely and easily accessible media, such as television, films, newspapers, music, comic books, and so on. Of course there are independent media outlets that might present a different perspective. For now, we're focusing on those that are most easily available, such as the major newspapers and magazines, Hollywood movies, popular social media sites, and so on.

Dominant cultures also shape education through textbooks and the training of educators and other professionals, as well as being reflected in our political and legal systems.

Let's give some examples of dominant ideas of gender from where we're located. Both of us have experienced challenges when navigating public restrooms or toilets, since far too often the only options are binary: male or female. Occasionally, family and/or accessible restrooms might be available. Even when those more inclusive options are available, we might get strange looks when accessing them without using a wheelchair or without a child in tow. Most schools also have only binary options for students. It is not uncommon for trans and gender-diverse young people to experience urinary tract infections because they're trying to avoid using restrooms that do not fit their needs, or because they might be actively threatened, or encounter violence there during the long school days. You may think that restrooms are a fairly specific example and that this situation only impacts trans and non-binary people. However, single parents often encounter difficulties when navigating these binary systems if their gender expression and/or identity do not match that of their child. People who need support from caregivers, in the absence of accessible restrooms, are often impacted as well. Cis people who do not appear to conform to societal expectations of gender also experience being challenged in public restrooms, such as cis women with increased facial and bodily hair because of Polycystic Ovarian Syndrome (PCOS) or cis men with increased breast tissue (gynecomastia).

The division of gender into the binary of men and women can also be seen in shops, for example, in how toys or clothing are organised. Changes are beginning to happen but these are still fairly limited to specific brands and stores. Generally, we still see toys labelled and advertised as being for girls or boys, with girls' toys tending to be pink or other pastel colours, and boys' toys displaying bolder, primary colours, such as red, blue, and yellow. Clothing follows a similar trend and is usually divided into boys/girls and men/women in stores. Some items of clothing, such as skirts and dresses, are still seen as the domain of femininity, rather than being more generally available, with make-up following a similar trend.

It is not just items and things that are labelled, divided, and advertised according to a binary idea of gender. Events such as league sports are also divided into men's and women's sports, with all that this entails, including which channel they are broadcast on and how much athletes are paid. In the United Kingdom one of the most prestigious tennis competitions, Wimbledon, still carries a smaller financial prize for female winners than for male winners, despite the established popularity of some of the main tennis stars who have competed and continue to compete there. Such disparities are often experienced by many people when it comes to the kind of jobs they feel are accessible to them and how much they get paid, with women and trans people, especially trans women of colour, generally earning far less than cis men, and often living close to or below the poverty line.

Reflection point: Gender where you live

Take a moment now to reflect on what the dominant culture looks like from where you are. Is it similar or different from what we've described? In what ways?

Exploring the past

These ideas might not be at all new to you. Mary Wollstonecraft wrote *A Vindication of the Rights of Woman* in 1792, and feminism continues to challenge gender stereotypes and their impact. Nevertheless, the idea of the gender binary has become so popular that many think it's the 'natural way of things' and an obvious consequence of our biology. Many people have challenged this idea across time and space, through activism, writing, research, and simply by living their lives.

As we mentioned in Section 1, gender is diverse, and as such not binary, not only in nature but also through history. For example, in the pre-Christian Roman Empire, the cult of the Phrygian deity Cybele was widespread. Her priestesses, called the Galli, were usually people who were assigned male at birth and presented in a feminine manner.

In the country many of us now call the United States, Indigenous people of various sovereign nations had many words to indicate multiple genders, and multiple gender expressions and roles were available to people, depending both on who they were and what the needs of the community were. Those roles were often, but not exclusively, sacred. The diversity of gender in Indigenous sovereign nations seemed alien to settler-colonisers who did not understand it and first developed offensive terms to describe this – for example, 'berdache' – before attempting to eradicate those expressions completely through genocide, separation of children from their families, and erasure of language and spiritual and cultural customs. As we've seen, the English-based term 'Two-Spirit' was created by Indigenous people of various nations to reclaim those lost identities, roles, and expressions. This term and identity is specific to Indigenous people, and those who have been adopted into such families and traditions.

Even in the history of Caucasian people in the United Kingdom and the United States, gender has not always been seen in the way it is today. For example, people are often surprised to learn that for some time there was assumed to be just one gender, with women being a slightly inferior kind of man. Also, as recently as a century ago, our current associations of gender with colour were the opposite, with blue being regarded as delicate and feminine, and pink as a more 'decided' colour, appropriate for boys.

These are just a few historical examples. There are many more, across many countries and times. We encourage you to do further research if you're interested in this topic. There's such a beautiful and rich tapestry of genders, historically and currently, all across the globe!

Exploring the present

While it's impossible in a short space to describe how rich and vast the gender landscape still is globally, it seems worthwhile to highlight here the resilience and continued existence of gender diversity. For example, hijras are still very much part of the current Indian social, cultural, and political landscapes, even though they have been impacted by colonialism. Hijras are assigned male at birth but identify and present as feminine. They have specific spiritual, cultural, and social roles, which were diminished and vilified during the colonial era. Kathoey are a similar – but distinct – group of people in Thailand. These kinds of experiences can be found in almost every corner of the globe, and include people of all bodies.

Gender diversity is not just the domain of trans and non-binary people. For example, some people assigned female at birth strongly identify as women and as butches. In African-American culture, some people identify as women and aggressives or studs.

Gender identities, expressions, roles, and experiences are not fixed and static. There is no 'pure' idea of gender, untouched by the impact of colonisation, globalisation, and technology. Learning about gender diversity in the past and present is not about trying to reclaim an idyllic past or exoticising specific bodies or cultural groups; rather, it is a reminder of the strength of diversity in human nature. No matter how hard we might have tried to suppress gender diversity, our varied identities, expressions, roles, and experiences keep re-emerging, claiming a little more space and room to breathe, reminding us that this is not a landscape that can be tamed and shaped into two parallel and distinct highways.

Reclaiming gender diversity

We have all been deeply impacted by colonisation in many ways, including gender. However, Indigenous people continue to actively experience intergenerational and cultural trauma in many aspects of their lives, including gender, in very specific ways, in many places around the globe. As you consider this landscape – which is vaster than you might have initially thought – and how it has many gradients where people negotiate identities, roles, and expressions in a myriad of ways, take a moment to consider how you may have also been impacted by the historical erasure of this array of genders. We'll discuss this further in the Sub-sections 2.2 and 2.3, as well as coming back to it later in the book.

2.2 GENDER STEREOTYPES

Now that we've considered the diversity of gender across time and space, let's think a bit more about the expectations around gender in our current place and time. In Section 2, as we've already said, we'll be focusing on Anglo-American culture. This is partly because of where we live, partly because it's the geographical area that this book is initially aimed at, and partly because – for all kinds of problematic reasons – that culture has a significant impact globally, and it's therefore worth giving it some critical attention.

FIGURE 2.1: MEDIA DEPICTIONS OF GENDER

However, it's important to be mindful that you – our reader – might well be familiar with other cultural contexts. If so, feel free to reflect on those too. Also, as we'll explore more in Section 3, even within one culture there is a whole load of diversity in terms of expectations around gender, depending on things like class, race, age, generation, faith, and geographical location.

So we're taking a very broad brush here to look at what we've been thinking of as dominant culture: the one that tends to tell the loudest and most bossy stories around gender. We'll come back later to explore some of the shyer stories, which we can also hear if we listen more carefully.

ACTIVITY: STEREOTYPICAL GENDER

Complete the table below to create lists of what is considered 'feminine', 'masculine', and 'androgynous' in the dominant culture where you are. Here we're asking you to think about the stereotypes around gender in wider culture, not what you actually think yourself. You might consider the roles, behaviours, emotions, and appearances that are seen as appropriate for each of these gender expressions. If you find it difficult to think of anything, consider how femininity, masculinity, and androgyny are represented in mainstream magazines, adverts, films, TV shows, and other mass media. Or you could reflect on how people around you talk about these things on an everyday basis.

Feminine	Masculine	Androgynous

We mentioned in the last section that gender stereotyping starts very early on in our lives, and generally along binary lines based on assumptions around masculinity and femininity. One piece of research that really highlighted this was the 'Baby X' study, back in the 1970s.[1] People were given a baby to hold, which was either dressed in pink or blue. The researchers found that people holding the blue-dressed babies played with them more roughly than the ones given the babies dressed in pink. People were also more likely to give the pink-dressed babies a doll to play with and the blue-dressed babies a truck. If the baby cried, people also tended to assume that they were angry if they were dressed in blue, or upset if they were dressed in pink. Other researchers have done this study again in more recent years and found similar results.[2]

---

1   Seavey, C.A., Katz, P.A. and Zalk, S.R. (1975) 'Baby X.' *Sex Roles 1*(2), 103–9.

2   Sidorowicz, L.S. and Lunney, G.S. (1980) 'Baby X revisited.' *Sex Roles 6*(1), 67–73.

People are often labelled and stigmatised from a young age if they don't match the stereotypes that are assumed for somebody who is assigned their sex at birth. For example, people who are assigned female may be called 'tomboys' or 'unladylike' if they are active, outspoken, or geeky, or if they're interested in things like sport, outdoor activities, or mechanics. People who are assigned male may be called 'sissy' or labelled with homophobic slurs if they are gentle, unsporty, or risk-avoidant, or if they're interested in things like appearance, dancing, or looking after people. Given how attuned children are to the world around them – and how much they generally want to belong and feel approved of by others, especially caregivers – such labelling can be very difficult, and the shame attached to it can remain with a person throughout their life.

Reflection point: The personal impact of gender stereotypes

Have you ever been affected by these stereotypes in a personal way? For example, you might think about experiences like bullying, how much you're paid in relation to colleagues, or whether you were allowed to play the sport of your choice as a child. This kind of reflection can be hard, so please remember to be gentle with yourself and notice any emotions that come up with curiosity. If it feels tough to remember, you might like to move away from the book for a while and do something calming and kind for yourself right now: maybe have a short stretch or a cup of your favourite hot drink.

As we've seen, gender stereotypes are everywhere in the world around us, every day of our lives. We see images of 'ideal' men and women on billboard adverts and in the pages of magazines. Films and TV programmes try to make us laugh by presenting people who don't quite match up to the 'manly men' and 'feminine women' that we've been taught to aspire to. Schoolyard and water cooler conversations frequently revolve around people who are bending or breaking the norms around gender: girls who play with the boys, boys who don't join in the football game, women who are 'too' sexually active, men who pay 'too much' attention to their appearance, or anybody who has shifted from their sex assigned at birth in any way.

Now that you've thought about your own experiences, take a read through the following examples of the ways in which other people experience being their gender in a very stereotyped world.

Multiple experiences: Being my gender in a stereotyped world

'For me it's very simple. I was bullied throughout school for not fitting in with the kind of femininity that was expected of me. I never wore the right clothes, read the right magazines, or liked the right bands; and make-up was completely beyond me. I soon learned that I had to conform if I wanted any friends, or a boyfriend.'

'As a male nurse I've had a lot of issues around gender. Even that term "male nurse" shows just how much everyone assumes that nursing is a female profession. Patients often assume I'm a doctor and laugh or look disappointed when they find out I'm not. In some departments the other nurses have regarded me with suspicion. In others, some have thought it was OK to make sexual comments about me all the time.'

'I've always enjoyed my femininity. I liked girly things growing up, and now I love buying clothes, dressing up, and going out dancing. However, I notice what a massive difference my gender makes at work, compared to my male colleagues. I often get treated as if I'm less clever. If I come up with an idea in a meeting, it gets ignored until one of the guys says the exact same thing and then everybody listens to him. And don't even get me started on how hard it is to get promoted.'

'Being an NB person, I get very used to being misgendered. Every time I go to the store or buy a drink in a café, it's all "Sir" or "Madam". Whichever way they go, it doesn't feel right to me. I deliberately choose shops where they have all the clothes on one floor and individual changing rooms. Going to the gym is a bit of a nightmare too because I've had hassle whichever changing room I've picked.'

In Sub-section 2.3 we'll think a bit more about the impact of these stereotypes and rigid rules around gender in all of our lives, particularly on our mental and physical health.

2.3 IMPACT OF GENDER STEREOTYPES

Rigid stereotypes around gender are bad for us all. You might already have considered some of the ways that stereotypes have impacted you personally in a negative way. Even when we fit some of the stereotypes fairly comfortably, others may be bad for us, as in the example from the woman who encountered misogyny and femmephobia in the workplace. And there can be problems if we hold onto the gender rules too tightly and they become less of a good fit over time. For example, many bromance films reflect that the kind of masculinity that worked well for a guy in his twenties can actually get in the way of the things that he might want to happen in his thirties and forties in terms of work and/or relationships.

Let's go through some of the ways in which gender stereotypes – especially when they are too rigidly policed – can also impact our mental and physical health, and put us at risk in other ways.

Intersex experience

First, for intersex people in many times and places, the rigid gender binary has meant that they are assigned male or female and given often unnecessary surgeries to make their bodies conform more to what is considered to be a male or female body. When this is done as a baby, a person has no capacity to consent. As well as the risk that the sex assignment will not fit with the person's later gender experience, some operations can leave them unable to feel genital arousal, which can have a detrimental impact on their later sex life. All of this can certainly take a toll on a person's mental health. For example, childhood surgeries can be traumatising, and it can be very tough indeed for people who are only told when they reach adulthood – or later, or never – that they're intersex.

Femininity

Whether a person is cis or trans, intersex or not, rigid ideals of femininity can have negative side effects for all women. For example, double standards around sexuality make it hard for women to be perceived as sexy 'enough' without being labelled a slut or slag. There's also the greater risk of sexual and domestic violence faced by women. In relation to health, women are particularly at risk for problems around body image and eating habits because of the narrow range of feminine bodies that are deemed physically attractive in dominant culture.

The higher rates of depression and anxiety amongst women have been linked to these beauty ideals, as well as to the fact that women are often encouraged to forge their identities around their relationships with others – for example, being likeable, or needing to find a husband, or being a good mother. This can lead to some women losing their sense of themselves, or struggling greatly when their life changes in ways that might take those identities away, such as divorce, separation, or their children leaving home.

Growing up, women are still less likely to see themselves reflected in wider culture as active agents in their own lives, compared to men. For example, the Bechdel test rates films on whether they have at least two female characters who have a conversation together at some point in the film about something other than a man.

You might want to think for a moment about whether you can think of many examples of such films. On the other hand, it can be much easier to find examples of films that have at least two male characters who have conversations with one another about several things other than women during the film, such as work, projects, sports, and so on.

Masculinity

Of course rigid gender stereotypes impact men negatively too, again whether those men are trans or cis, intersex or not. You might have noticed in some of our examples so far that men who are seen as in any way feminine can be policed even more heavily than women who are masculine. In a world where masculinity is often seen as the ideal way of being, or even the norm, there can be some understanding that those who are not men might want to be masculine, but very little understanding that somebody assigned male at birth might want to move away from stereotypical masculinity.

If women are sometimes viewed as childlike, out of control, or as objects of desire because their identities are bound up with others, men are often viewed as needing to be responsible, in control, hard, and strong. This can make it very difficult for men to admit when they're struggling, or to express the full range of emotions including fear and sadness. Avoiding or suppressing those feelings takes a heavy toll on a person's mental health, although men may be a lot less likely to seek help when they are struggling. This has been linked to the higher rates of suicide and drug and alcohol problems among men.

Men are often encouraged to externalise, rather than internalise, their struggles, through fighting or other forms of aggression. When they do act in such ways, they're often more likely to be seen as 'bad' than 'mad', whereas for women it's often the reverse. So men are more likely to be convicted of crimes and sent to prison, as well as being more likely to be the victims of violent crimes. On the other hand, women are likely to have longer and sometimes harsher convictions when tried for a crime, probably because committing a crime goes against our stereotypes of femininity as being nurturing and compliant.

Men are more likely than women to die in every decade of life, and that may be linked to various factors, such as the kinds of jobs they are expected to take, their reluctance to seek help for mental and physical health problems, and their greater likelihood of being involved in violent incidents, including wars and criminal behaviours.

Non-binary experience

Rigid gender stereotypes are bad for men, they're bad for women, and clearly they are bad for anybody who falls outside of the gender binary. Non-binary and genderqueer people are often completely invisible because everyone assumes that a person is either a man or a woman. They have high rates of mental health problems due to this experience of invisibility, erasure, and frequent questioning of their gender, or misgendering.

This also takes a toll on their physical health, as all mental health difficulties do. As we said earlier, non-binary and genderqueer people can experience physical problems due to struggling to find toilets they can use, and it is often hard for them to find medical professionals who will treat them affirmatively, which can mean that they avoid going to the doctor when they need to. Non-binary and genderqueer people also suffer high rates of suicidal feelings and physical and sexual violence due to transphobic reactions.

Intersections

Of course all of the impacts that we've spoken about here are rather broad brushstrokes about women, men, and non-binary people in general. When we get specific, we notice that things are very different within various groups and communities. This is the idea of intersectionality that we'll come back to again and again throughout the book. For example, age makes a difference. Men who've grown up in recent decades have faced the particular challenge of persisting stereotypes of the hard, strong breadwinner, while in reality 'traditional' male jobs and roles that would allow them to live out these stereotypes have continued to decline. Race comes into it too, of course, since we know that Black men are by far the most likely people to be victims of violent crime and to be criminalised. Sexuality is another intersection – for example, gay men are more likely to struggle with body image issues than straight men. Also, of course, trans men and women can face all of the issues that cis men and women face, with the added elements of transphobia, such as people questioning their gender, or attacking them for it. We'll say a lot more about intersections, and the ways in which they combine, in Sections 3 and 4.

The following examples give you a bit more of a flavour of how gender stereotypes can intersect with other aspects of our identities and experiences. We've included a few more examples of women and non-binary people here because we focused more on men and masculinity in the last paragraph.

Multiple experiences: The impact of gender stereotypes

'I'm genderqueer but I'm very aware that I'm fortunate to be living in a time and place where people get that. There's gender diversity in my cultural background, so my family have got their heads around it now. Half my friends are non-binary too. I work for an LGBT charity, and while they're not perfect by any means, at least I know that everyone I meet there has heard of the concept. And we have non-gendered bathrooms at work.'

'As a young Black woman, I don't feel that I can come out as bisexual in my workplace. I already get people sexualising me all the time: touching me inappropriately or assuming that I'm available just for being a Black woman. Adding bisexuality to that would make it even worse. Having to stay in the closet takes a real toll on my mental health.'

'I'm a woman in my fifties and I'm disabled. To a lot of the world that means I'm just not seen as a sexual being. And I really like sex! I'm so sick of the fact that only young women without physical disabilities are seen as sexy. Why would we limit women in this way?'

'I'm a fat working-class queer femme and proud of it. But people have such a problem with that. In a lot of places it's not seen as "feminine" to be fat, or to be loud and mouthy, or to be attracted to women, and I'm all of those things. And when I go into LGBT spaces, people question whether I'm really queer because I embrace my femininity. I can't win!'

Reflection point: The impact of living your gender in a stereotyped world

Think a bit about the impact of living your gender within your wider world with all of its stereotypes. You might want to consider the impact on the following:

− physical health

− mental health

− housing situation

− economic situation

− your close relationships

− how you're seen in the world: for example, whether people like you are regarded as threatening or not, or are seen as having agency over their lives or not.

Again, remember to be kind with yourself when reflecting on something like this, which can be tough. It's always OK to step away for a while and come back later, or to wait for a time when you're feeling strong enough.

Interestingly, and possibly unsurprisingly given everything we've spoken about here, research has found that the people who seem to be most healthy in several ways are those who are able to be quite flexible around their genders, that is, adopting behaviours and roles that are associated with masculinity or femininity or androgyny, depending on the situation. Given that this is the case, it seems particularly sad that dominant culture still tries to put people into rigid boxes when it comes to gender. Let's think more about how well you – and the people you know – actually fit those boxes, and what options are available if you – or they – do not.

But, before that, take a moment to breathe...

Breathe.

Please slow down. You don't need to grit your teeth and rush through the book in one go. It's OK to put it down and pick it up again later, at a better time.

Here are some ideas for things to do if you're struggling with difficult, uncomfortable or unpleasant feelings right now:

Make a cup of coffee, or tea, focusing first on making it, then drinking it. Take time to feel the warmth of the cup, to take in the smell, and to savour the taste.

Think of a place or time where or when you felt particularly safe and happy. If there's no such place and time, it's OK to fantasise and imagine what a happy and safe place would be like. Let yourself spend a meaningful amount of time with this memory or fantasy. What do you notice with all the senses available to you? Have a warm bath, take a long shower, or visit a favourite body of water near you, such as a lake, river, or pond. Notice anything that might shift in your body as you take care of yourself.

Breathe some more, and when you feel more comfortable, or neutral, let's continue…

2.4 MASCULINITIES, FEMININITIES, ANDROGYNIES, AND BEYOND

By now, you've probably figured out that we're somewhat biased towards the idea of gender liberation! Let's talk for a moment about what we mean by this. Sometimes people think that gender liberation is about doing away with gender altogether and moving towards androgyny for everyone. This is definitely not our intention! We'd like to see a world where everyone is free to express their gender, or genders, in ways that feel authentic to them in that moment – for example, one gender expression might be different from in the past; it might change in the future; or it might stay the same over time.

We would like this freedom to be for everybody, for everyone to feel safe, especially trans feminine people of colour, who are currently experiencing the most violence globally because of transmisogyny (that is, the specific fear and hate that some people, and the dominant culture, often hold against trans people and femininity) and its intersection with racism. When we talk about gender liberation, we're dreaming of a world where people can explore the vast gender landscape without fear or negative consequences. Maybe this seems a little idealistic, but most liberation starts from a seed and we feel the seed of gender liberation has been planted for some time – it has blossomed in the past and it might indeed bloom again.

In the meantime, while continuing to dream, we'd like to encourage you to explore how you relate to the gender landscape, including stereotypes and their impact. After this, we'll turn our attention to current gender options available to you in the United Kingdom and the United States.

ACTIVITY: WHERE DO YOU FIT IN THE DOMINANT CULTURE VIEWS OF GENDER?

For this activity, we'd like you to refer back to the lists you created in Sub-section 2.2 about gender stereotypes relating to masculinity, femininity, and androgyny. Consider your list and then notice the following:

— Do you fit any column perfectly? If not, where are the places you do not fit, and why?

— Do people you know fit the columns perfectly? If not, in what ways and why?

— Does anyone fit better in a different column than what you would have expected? How so?

Please take a few moments to jot down your thoughts in a journal or notebook. Alternatively, you can choose to discuss those issues with a trusted group of friends and compare your ideas about gender.

Current gender options in the United Kingdom and the United States

We mention at various times in this book that our ideas of gender have changed, and continue to change over time and across space. What are the options currently in the places where we are located as authors, and where you're most likely to be as readers? Once again, please approach this topic with caution. Some of these things change all the time, and they might already have done so between the time we wrote this and the time you read it. Please refer to the resources list at the end of this section for guidance on where to look for the most up-to-date information.

Given that gender identities, expressions, and roles are so multifaceted, they touch many aspects of our lives (and gender is biopsychosocial, so it literally touches every facet of who we are). Below, we address some of the main ones you might be wondering about, that is, what your gender options are: legally, socially, medically, relationally, educationally, and professionally. This is not an exhaustive list but rather a point from which to start. Feel free to add other domains relevant to your life to this list!

Legal gender options

In most countries, people are assigned a name and gender on their birth certificate. Those names and gender markers then usually follow a person throughout their life, and are used on documents such as passports, tax identification numbers, social security cards in the United States, driver licences, educational certificates, and many other official papers. Most of the time, these are also the markers and names we have to use on important financial documents – for example, when applying for credit and debit cards.

It's possible to change both your name and gender marker in many countries, including the ones where we live. However, different rules apply for each. For example, it is generally much simpler, and there are fewer requirements linked, to changing one's name. Changing gender markers is usually more challenging, and it might have more requirements connected with it, such as having made significant body modifications.

The requirements in the United States change from state to state and are not only linked to your citizenship status, but also determined by the state of your birth. For example, if you were born in Minnesota, you do not need to have made any body modifications to change your gender marker; however, if you were born in Florida, you would need to have made significant surgical body modifications before being allowed a legal gender marker change.

Not everyone who wants to is able to change their name and/or gender marker. Cost might be an issue, or citizenship status – for example, if someone is an undocumented immigrant. Also not everyone wants to change their name or gender marker legally. For many non-binary people, changing gender marker might seem pointless as the options currently available in most countries are only male or female. For others, changing gender markers can be important due to safety concerns, even if the changed marker might not truly reflect their identity.

Social gender options

As well as being given a legal name and gender marker, people around us often interact with us in particular ways because of our gender identities, expressions, and roles. For example, people might use specific pronouns to refer to us, such as 'she', 'they', 'he', 'per', or 'ze'. They might also use titles that many people consider gendered, such as 'dad', 'mom', 'uncle', 'aunt', 'brother', 'sister', 'wife', or 'husband', as well as 'Miss', 'Madam', 'Sir', 'Ms', and so on.

It can be challenging to ask people around us to use a different name, pronoun, or title for us. Some of you might have used a nickname for a long time, or have had the experience of asking someone not to use a specific abbreviation of your name (e.g. 'Babs' for Barbara) because you don't like it or because you have negative associations with that abbreviation. Some people might also have experienced asking people to change the use of their name or title after marriage or divorce.

If you feel that a name, pronoun, or title no longer fits you, it's OK to ask people around you to use a different one. For trans people, this is sometimes seen as part of their social transition; that is, they're changing the way they interact socially with the world around them, and the language used to refer to them might change as a consequence. However, it's also OK to change some things and not others. For example, one of the authors (Alex) is a parent. His child has decided that they like calling him both 'Mamma' and 'Daddy Two'. They always use the right pronouns for Alex and don't think of being a mother as a gendered role. In fact, they often celebrate both parents and people with a close caregiver role on Mother's Day, in the spirit rather than the literal meaning of the holiday. You get to decide what social gender options seem right for you!

Medical gender options

You also get to decide what options you might have medically, even though there might be conditions attached to whatever medical intervention you might be seeking related to your gender identity and/or expression. Some medical options that are linked to sex and gender are: hormonal treatment, chest reconstruction surgery, hysterectomy, vaginoplasty, phalloplasty, and tracheal shaving. When trans people undergo some of these body modifications, this is usually seen as part of what is called their medical transition. Of course, not every trans person seeks body modification. They might not want to, or they might not be able to undergo any changes due to financial or health obstacles.

Medical gender options are not only the domain of trans people. For example, many people might experience needing to have a hysterectomy or chest reconstruction surgery, due to health issues such as cancer, back pain, or endometriosis, or because of discomfort with their appearance. They might also use hormonal treatments to regulate early onset of puberty and reproductive cycles, to alter their bodily appearance, or to deal with changing hormone levels during the menopause.

How accessible medical gender options are is very dependent on the healthcare system in the country where you live. For example, in the United Kingdom, where there is a universal healthcare system, those options might be more accessible, but there might be much longer waiting times, as well as several conditions to meet. In the United States, the Affordable Care Act has increased access to medical options for many people; however, significant barriers remain. Those might still vary from state to state, and if someone is uninsured, underinsured, undocumented, or has a health insurance plan that requires a high deductible (excess), medical gender options might not be at all available. This Act is also subject to the flux of who is in political office and it may or may not still be in place by the time you read this. In some places charitable and activist groups have been set up to help people to access private health care if they're unable to go through other routes.

Relational systems and gender options

Sometimes relational systems, such as family of origin, children and grandchildren, partners, and so on can be the hardest to navigate when it comes to gender options. Even though there is increased awareness of the broader gender landscape, those close to us might feel as if they know us best – even better than we know ourselves.

Navigating our gender identities, expressions, and roles, and sharing our experiences with the people we are closest to, can seem risky and make us feel very vulnerable, maybe even too vulnerable. Sometimes, it might actually be unsafe to share our gender identities, expressions, roles, and experiences with those closest to us, especially if we're isolated and have no immediate support options, not only emotionally, but also economically and geographically. It is up to you how you navigate gender in your relationships, and it might well be different from relationship to relationship and from place to place. We'll come back to some aspects of this topic in much more depth in Section 6.

Educational and employment gender options

Education and employment are also areas in which you might feel particularly vulnerable expressing your gender. Because of the power dynamics you find yourself in (e.g. as a student or an employee), it might not always feel safe for you to be open about your identities, expressions, roles, or experiences. For example, there might be no private space for you to express milk at work when you are breastfeeding, and this issue may never have been brought up at your workplace because it is mostly dominated by cis men who have never had to think about it. Or you might be the first person to come out as trans in your school. Both the United Kingdom and the United States have some legal protections in place when it comes to gender. However, in the United States those legal protections might vary from state to state, so make sure you get appropriate legal advice about your rights!

Reflection point: Gender options

Take a moment to think about what your gender options are where you live. Do you feel you would like to have further options to fully express your gender? What would those be? If you notice challenging emotions and/or sensations arise, please take a break, get some support, and remember to be very gentle with yourself. All these topics can bring up difficult emotions. It's OK to go slow, ask for support, and take as many breaks as you need.

REMEMBER: If these issues feel somewhat overwhelming, don't worry, we'll come back to all of them at various points in this book! We've also included some recommended resources for you below.

FURTHER RESOURCES

You can read about Mary Wollstonecraft's *Rights of Women* in:

- Craciun, A. (2013) *Mary Wollstonecraft's A Vindication of the Rights of Woman.* Abingdon/London: Routledge.

You can read more about the diversity of gender identities, roles, expressions, and experiences over time and across cultures in the following books:

- Feinberg, L. (1996) *Transgender Warriors: Making History from Joan of Arc to Dennis Rodman.* Boston, MA: Beacon Press.

- Herdt, G. (2012) *Third Sex, Third Gender: Beyond Sexual Dimorphism in Culture and History.* Cambridge, MA: Zone Books.

If you want to read more about the way that gender is represented in wider culture, and the impact this has, the following two books are great:

- Gauntlett, D. (2008) *Media, Gender and Identity: An Introduction.* London: Routledge.

- Gill, R. (2007) *Gender and the Media.* Cambridge: Polity.

These films and books are helpful explorations of representations of femininities and masculinities particularly:

- *Miss Representation* (2011) (documentary written, directed, and produced by Jennifer Siebel Newsom). Available at www. therepresentationproject.org/film/miss-representation, accessed on 18 May 2017.

- *The Mask You Live In* (2015) (documentary written, directed, and produced by Jennifer Siebel Newsom). Available at www.therepresentationproject.org/film/the-mask-you-live-in, accessed on 18 May 2017.

- *Straightlaced: How Gender's Got Us All Tied Up* (2009) (documentary written and directed by Debra Chasnoff, produced by Debra Chasnoff and Sue Chen). Listed at www.imdb.com/title/tt1404412, accessed on 8 June 2017.

- Penny, L. (2011) *Meat Market.* London: Zero.

- Urwin, J. (2016) *Man Up.* London: Icon Books.

The following online resource is also useful, especially if you are thinking about the impact of Whiteness and settler-colonialism on gender:

- https://publishbiyuti.org/decolonisingtransgender101

YOUR GENDER BACKGROUND

We promised you that we were going to get more personal in Section 3... Here not only can you further reflect on your gender history, but also we invite you to notice how your own gender history weaves with the larger stories around us: those social, cultural, political, geographical, and economic stories we mentioned in Sections 1 and 2. In those sections, we introduced a lot of ideas about gender and how it intersects with other aspects of our identity; also, how people might be impacted by notions of gender in dominant culture. You may already have more ideas about how you relate to gender than when you started this book.

For now, we'd like you to take a trip back in time. First we'll revisit the time of your birth. What sex were you assigned at this important moment in your story and what was the impact? Then we'll explore all the ways in which your gender was shaped by other aspects of your position growing up, such as your geographical location, language, class, race, ethnicity, religion/spirituality, disability status, and so on. After spending some time at those intersections, we'll pay attention to what has shifted, and what hasn't, over our lives. Finally, we'll discuss why it's important to have some familiarity with our gender stories, and we'll give you some ideas for how to tell and/or re-tell your own gender story.

You may want to have your journal or notebook with you for this section, as there'll be plenty of activities! If you're worried about this, take a breath and give yourself permission to just read through the section at first, if that feels more comfortable. Please remember that each activity is an invitation – you can accept it, refuse it, come back to it, or modify it to fit your needs. There's no need to do anything you don't want to do, at least while reading this book. There's plenty of that in our everyday lives already!

3.1 'IT'S A ...': THE SEX YOU WERE ASSIGNED AT BIRTH

Let's start with a refresher from Sections 1 and 2. If you remember, we talked there about the sex that people are assigned at birth, explaining that in the United Kingdom, the United States, and many other countries, babies are generally deemed to be either 'boys' or 'girls' by the doctors, parents, and/or others who are around them when they're born. Also babies are still also often operated on at an early age if their body doesn't conform to what's expected of a boy or a girl, in order to shape their genitals into a vulva, vagina, and clitoris, or a penis and testes.

Fortunately, things are improving for intersex people, as many clinicians and psychologists are now working with intersex activists to move towards more of an informed-consent model in situations where surgeries aren't medically necessary. This involves waiting until children are old enough to be included in decisions about any changes that might be made to their bodies.

Intergenerational gender issues

Things have certainly improved from the past when intersex people were sometimes institutionalised, or even left to die. Jane Czyzselska, the editor of *DIVA* magazine, writes powerfully about her own family history where a decision was made to focus on keeping a non-intersex baby alive at the expense of an intersex twin, who died. Such events can result in intergenerational traumas and losses that echo down the generations, as well as leading to secrecies and silences around certain aspects of gender within families.

Such histories of intergenerational trauma around gender don't just happen in relation to intersex people. Other sadly common examples include family histories of a gender or sexually diverse family member being cast out, forced into some form of 'treatment', or leaving because of the abuse they received. Gender politics can also result in family conflicts, losses, and traumas – for example, where older generations choose to treat sons and daughters, and their families, differently in their wills due to their gender. There are situations too where children are forced or pressured into marriage because of their gender. And there are occasions where different ideas around feminism or gender equality cause rifts between generations or siblings. Again, such traumas don't just affect the generation that they happen in – their impact often ripples down for generations to come.

ACTIVITY: INTERGENERATIONAL ATTITUDES AROUND GENDER

If it's a safe enough thing for you to do in your family, you might want to talk to family members about the understandings of gender that were around them growing up, and how they passed these on or decided to shift away from them when bringing up the next generation. If you wanted to, you could even build up a kind of gender family tree of the gender identities, roles, expressions, and experiences that were present in each generation going back as far as you're aware. You could do this based on conversations or just on your own recollections. If adoption is part of your history, this might involve reflecting on the differences between your adoptive family and family of origin – if you have that information.

Once again, please go easy on yourself – and others – with this kind of activity. Not all family members will necessarily be comfortable discussing gender in these ways, and some may want to keep aspects of their experiences and history private. The informed-consent model is useful here: letting people know that you're interested in having that kind of conversation if they are, but that it is fine not to as well, and then letting them come to you if they're keen. We've included some good resources at the end of the section about how to communicate in families if there are gender tensions that you'd like to be able to talk about more openly.

How does our sex assigned at birth impact us?

The sex that we're assigned at birth can impact our life course from the beginning. Remember the Baby X study from Sub-section 2.2, which showed that the people around us start treating us differently, depending on our birth-assigned sex, from the moment we're born? Alex witnessed first-hand how people can react very differently to the same child, based on their gender assumptions. During the first couple of years of his child's life, Alex dressed them in various ways: sometimes in what would be considered to be boys' clothes and other times in what would be considered to be girls' clothes. This was due not only to trying to save money while raising a family by maximising on hand-me-down clothes from friends, but also to not putting too much weight on the whole boy/girl clothes issues for babies and toddlers.

Alex found it fascinating to notice how people would use different adjectives to describe the same baby – for example, 'handsome' when people thought they were a boy, and 'beautiful' or 'pretty' when people thought they were a girl. People would also remark on the child's strength if they thought they were a boy, and how shy they were if they thought they were a girl. People's facial expressions, voice, and pitch too would change according to these assumptions! Of course, this stopped happening once Alex's child could speak and express themselves with more agency.

We'll come back to this later. For now, it's just worth considering quite how much of an impact all of these micro-moments of gendering can have on a developing kid. This is also a good example of how gender is clearly biopsychosocial. People related to Alex's baby based on social assumptions, which influenced how they were reading clues, such as clothes, regardless of the child's biological make-up. In case you are worried about the psychological impact of such an experiment, we would like to reassure you that Alex's child grew up to have a clear and strong sense of self, including their gender identity! However, they are also not limited in their gender roles and expressions by gender stereotypes, giving them a healthy range of possibilities.

This might even go back further than our birth if our parents had an ultrasound. Meg-John remembers how difficult some of their family members found it when Meg-John suggested that it might be good not to greet a baby with this kind of gendered treatment from the word go. Their mum pointed out that even if you don't knit baby clothes in pink or blue, in British and American culture you still have to decide which side of a cardigan to put the buttons on depending on gender!

Here are some more examples of the ways in which sex assigned at birth can have an impact right from the start, and throughout our lives.

Multiple experiences: The impact of sex assigned at birth

'Growing up I always noticed that my parents and other adults they knew seemed a bit "off" with me. They seemed to treat me a bit differently to my sisters and to the other girls I knew. I remember wondering whether there might be something wrong with me, and that sense of wrongness stayed with me throughout my life, especially when I realised that I couldn't experience sexual arousal with a partner in the way that most of my friends did. It was only in my thirties that a doctor mentioned my intersex status to me. She'd assumed that I already knew!

It took me a long time, and lots of therapy, to get over what my family did to me by keeping that a secret, and to get comfortable in my femininity without questioning whether I was a "proper" woman.'

'In my family and culture, birth-assigned sex marks you out on a completely different life course. Those assigned male wear different clothes, are educated in different ways, worship in different areas, and have very different life expectations on them than those who're assigned female. I didn't really question this as a kid: I just followed the path set out for me. But as an adult I've definitely made choices to buy into some aspects of the gender path and not others. Looking into my faith in more depth, my view is that a lot of this stuff is more cultural than religious, because the early texts definitely have room for more gender diversity than is currently allowed.'

'We're trying to raise our kid gender neutral. We both received so much crap about masculinity and femininity growing up that we really wanted to do things differently as parents. So we picked a gender-neutral name for Pat and we're using gender-neutral pronouns for them too, until they get to the point where they want to choose their own pronouns, or maybe change their name. You wouldn't believe the amount of grief we get from other parents. It's like imposing gender stereotypes on your kid is fine, but trying to keep things open is seen as an act of abuse!'

'As a trans man I certainly suffered from the sex I was assigned at birth. It didn't fit my experience. The older I got, the deeper the sense that people had got something wrong. In my forties I transitioned and I've been so much happier ever since. However, when I look at kids transitioning in elementary or even high school now, sometimes I get sad, sometimes angry. It is hard to imagine how different my life would have been if I could have been myself sooner – how much pain I would have been spared, and who I could have been if I hadn't spent all this time struggling to be someone I was not.'

Reflection point: Impact of sex assigned at birth on you

Think through the expectations that people around you had because of the sex that you were assigned at birth. How did this shape you, especially as a child? And in what ways is it still impacting you today?

3.2 INTERSECTIONS

We discussed earlier how all aspects of our gender, identities, expressions, and roles do not develop in isolation. We are shaped by language, family of origin, the place where we're born, our socioeconomic status, race, ethnicity, religion, disability, and more. In addition to those influences, we are also shaped by our own experiences, as we've explored earlier.

Next, we'd like you to think about all aspects of your identities, so that you can better understand who, what, and how your gender identities, expressions, roles, and experiences were shaped. For now, we'll focus on those intersections you were born into. Later we'll move on to how those might have changed as you go through life. We believe it's important to know where we're coming from in relation to gender and all aspects of our identities. That's because when we know where we've come from, we can start to become better acquainted with the complex tapestry of power, oppression, and privilege we experienced growing up.

Power, oppression, and privilege

Power, oppression, and privilege can seem like loaded words, especially when focusing on your own experiences growing up, so let's take a moment to briefly define what we mean. We've already mentioned how in dominant culture there are bossier and shyer stories. Those stories that shape our legal, social, and cultural systems have power on both collective and individual levels. Their power is sneaky in many ways. For example, one of the powers of dominant stories is to appear as if they're just 'what's normal' for everyone. That's where privilege comes in. Privilege means being born into something that fits so well with the powerful stories where we live that things seem 'natural and easy' in specific areas of our lives, thereby giving us an unearned advantage.

We mentioned earlier the example of cis privilege. Another example is being born White in the United Kingdom or the United States. There is privilege in this because our social and cultural structures implicitly give power and advantages to White people. In the United States, White privilege might look like not being stopped by the police while driving, something that happens so frequently to Black people that it's referred to as 'driving while Black'. The latter experience can be dangerous as it often leads to unbidden police brutality and in too many cases even death. This is also an example of oppression. Oppression happens when people have set up society in such a way that some are systematically disadvantaged, while others start from an easier position and have fewer obstacles to overcome to reach the same goals or deal with the same systems.

Because our lives are multifaceted, we often experience power and privilege in some areas and oppression in others. We don't have a single identity but rather various identities, roles, and experiences in relation to domains like gender, race, age, class, and so on. Those identities, roles, and experiences together are far greater and more complex than the sum of their parts. Intersectionality is a model that enables us to look at this complexity. As we mentioned at the start of the book, intersectionality was first introduced in the late 1980s by Kimberlé Crenshaw, a Black legal scholar in the United States, to describe the experiences of Black women in the criminal system and how they differed from those of White women, or Black men. The idea of intersectionality has a strong influence on us as authors. However, it's important to remember that it was born from Black feminism due to the marginalisation of Black voices within a largely White, Anglo-American feminist movement. It is also important to remember that all Black women, including trans women, are often most impacted by the combination of transphobia, misogyny, and racism in dominant culture, in all aspects of their lives.

Now that we've explained where some of our ideas come from, let's go back to our promise of looking at personal gender stories more closely.

Intersections of gender: At the beginning

What does it mean when we talk about gender being shaped by different aspects of our identities and by experiences? To better illustrate this, we'll use examples from our own lives before asking you to reflect on your own. In these examples, we've reflected on what we experienced growing up.

In Sub-section 3.3 we'll focus more on shifts and changes over time.

Meg-John's example and reflections

Meg-John drew this picture reflecting on their intersections.

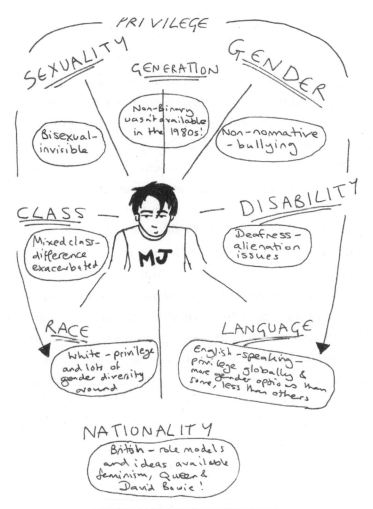

FIGURE 3.1: MEG-JOHN'S INTERSECTIONS

MEG-JOHN REFLECTS...

When drawing this picture of some of the key intersections that impacted my gender growing up, I was thinking about privilege. The aspects of my experience at the top are ones where I might think of myself as less privileged than other people who fitted in better to what was seen as 'normal', for example, or who had more options available to them. The aspects that are level with the picture of me are ones that are pretty complicated. In some ways I was very privileged having a middle-class upbringing, but my mixed-class status of having one parent from a working-class background and one from an upper-middle-class background made it difficult to fit into a largely working-class school where the available options for femininity were very different to those in my family of origin. Also having parents who came from the south of England meant that I didn't have a northern accent, which intersected with my gender and my hearing problems as a child to make me quite isolated in that context.

Down at the bottom of my picture are some of the areas in which I was definitely privileged in relation to my gender. My race, nationality, and language all mean that I had lots of options available to me that aren't available to many people. Coupled with class expectations, generation, and economic privilege, this meant that I was able to go through the university system for free, where, eventually, I began to learn about gender in an academic way, which helped me to understand it better on a personal level.

Alex's example and reflections

Alex drew this mind map like a web to reflect on his intersections.

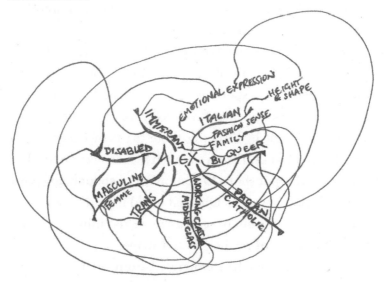

FIGURE 3.2: ALEX'S INTERSECTIONS

ALEX REFLECTS...

When drawing this picture, I was intimidated. I am not much of an artist, so I focused on words. I started out with an idea of branches and sub-branches, then realised it was getting too complex and started to sum up more. I first wrote Italian because that's where I was born. It was actually a little more complicated as I was born and brought up in Rome, a large, metropolitan city, while spending all my holidays in a small town in Sicily with my great-aunts, as well as spending much of my time with my maternal grandmother, who was also Sicilian. Ideas of gender in Rome and small-town Sicily were quite different. In one, I felt a degree of freedom of expression; in the other, I was not allowed to walk alone with boys, and there was more policing of my clothes and mannerisms. For example, I had to watch not sitting with my knees splayed, which my great-aunt and grandmother found unfeminine behaviour.

Fashion was a big part of my gender growing up. I felt I was in drag, and almost liked seeing how I could play with femininity while also sporting very short hair. I also feel that the way I express my emotions is very much about where I was born, and that it fits better there than any other Anglo places I have lived in. There's so much more to say on this but I'm trying to keep it short! One more word about being born in Italy: I'm an average height that could fit with any gender there, but I am definitely seen as more feminine in Anglo countries because of my height and shape.

My grandmother had emigrated from Sicily to Rome, which is like a different country in many ways, and I was surrounded by stories of immigration to Germany and the United States when I visited Sicily, including those of my great-uncles who had all moved after the Second World War. These too shaped my gender as it seemed clear that masculine people were typically the ones moving to find a better life, while women either followed them or stayed behind. I was also brought up Catholic but in a very Sicilian way, which is much more resonant with my current Pagan spirituality than with the Anglo-Germanic Catholicism I later encountered.

I was brought up in a working-class environment by a family where some people had come from more middle-class backgrounds and others aspired to them. This was often confusing growing up, even though it was clear that education was prized by all regardless, albeit not too much education for girls as it would 'spoil our eyes'. Having a gender that didn't clearly fit anywhere was also interesting. I had both masculine and feminine characteristics growing up, and it was clear that some were nurtured by some people in my family, and others were not. However, the same characteristics were valued by one person, and not another, so this was confusing too!

Finally, I feel I had educational privilege growing up but also experienced some hardships and humiliations around living in the 'wrong' neighbourhood – especially in middle and high school – as well as clearly being from Southern Italy, with darker skin, eyes, and colouring than some of my peers. In middle school, one of my teachers suggested I shouldn't go on to college as I didn't seem to be very bright. This was at a time when I was being bullied and therefore kept more to myself. My family, though, believed in me and had created a story of me being smart, which definitely served me as I went through my life.

This is only the beginning...

Please note that these reflections are but a glimpse at this point in time! After drawing our pictures, both of us immediately noticed things that we'd missed. After writing our reflections, we also felt we could have written more or less on various things, and we highlighted how, over time, all those stories shimmered and changed. We're not asking you to create a fixed picture, but rather to take a snapshot of your thoughts about the beginning of your story, looking back from this point in time.

ACTIVITY: YOUR INTERSECTIONS GROWING UP

Now that you've read our reflections and diagrams, take a moment to create your own. Take some time to reflect on which aspects of your identities and background shaped and intersected with your gender growing up. You can draw, make a mind map, or do whatever makes sense to you. Notice how both of us did this activity quite differently. There is no right or wrong way – just go for it!

Reflection point: Your own, and other people's, gender intersections

Now that you've thought about your own experiences of gender growing up, notice if there are gender experiences, identities, expressions, and roles that are less familiar to you because of your own intersections. For example, there might be genders you have had little or no contact with growing up, due to lack of contact with people of different ages, classes, cultures, disabilities, and so on.

Let's take a breath…

Thinking about things like power, oppression, and privilege can trigger all sorts of feelings, sensations, thoughts, and memories.

If you're noticing tightness in your body, shallow breathing, or temperature changes (e.g. feeling warmer or colder not due to outside factors), it's probably a good time to take a break.

Taking a break might be a good idea even if you don't notice any of these things!

You might want to take a moment to tune in and see whether you'd like to stretch. Maybe you'd like to listen to some of your favourite music, do some colouring, or take a nap. Too often we don't let ourselves rest or play enough. Can you give yourself permission to take care of yourself for the next 30 minutes? If that's too long, how about taking 10 minutes for yourself? Even 1 minute is better than nothing!

When you're ready to continue, the book will still be here for you…

3.3 GROWING UP GENDERED: LEARNING OVER TIME

Something that we touched on back in Section 1 was the idea that our gender is not fixed over time. Remember how we considered how we change at every level across our lifespan? To refresh your memory, biologically our bodies and brains change as we grow physically, learn new things, and lay down memories. Psychologically we develop different understandings and strengthen or weaken our habits over time, as well as having experiences that alter the direction of our lives in big and small ways. Socially we're exposed to different ideas, people, and relationships in a culture that's also ever changing. Given that gender is biopsychosocial, all of these things shape our ways of being in the world in relation to gender and in many other respects. Additionally, as we saw, all of these things interact with each other in complex ways.

Now that we're focusing in on your gender background, let's think some more about how your gender developed over time, particularly during your childhood and teenage years.

Fixity and fluidity

A really important point to make about this is that not every aspect of gender is fluid for everybody. Rather, most of us experience some parts of our gender as fixed and stable, and other parts as fluid and flexible; there is also a huge range of gender experiences in-between. For example, our gender identity might stay the same throughout our lives, but we take on roles that are strongly associated with different genders at different points in time; a case in point is a woman who fights on the frontline in the military during her twenties and becomes a stay-at-home mum in her thirties. Or it might be that our experience of our gender is consistent but we express it in different ways at different points in our lives. For example, a guy might experience himself very much as masculine throughout his life: as a boy he expresses this through playing sports; as a teenager he expresses it through getting drunk with his friends and being a player; as a young adult he expresses it through trying to do well in his career and to settle down with a partner; and as an elderly man he expresses it through going on fishing holidays with his male friends. He probably also wears different clothes and different hairstyles at each different age too.

Here are a couple of our own examples: Alex reflects that his daughter has kept a pretty stable gender identity over the last decade, as a girl, but that her expression of her femininity has changed a lot, from being into pink things, dresses, and skirts, to mostly wearing jeans and hoodies. For Meg-John, in some ways the opposite is the case. A lot of their gender expression has stayed fairly constant for the past decade. In fact, some of the clothes in their wardrobe date back at least that far! However, their gender identity has changed from woman to non-binary person.

Another important point to make is that just because an aspect of gender is fluid for somebody does not mean that they could easily choose for it to be otherwise. Often we might observe aspects of our gender shifting over time, but experience these changes as a path that we need to go down. It wouldn't be easy – or even possible – to take another road, and if we are denied the possibility of going down that path, we can end up feeling a great deal of pain and discomfort. We need to be very careful not to give the impression that people could ever simply choose for their gender – or their gender journey – to be other than it is.

Let's take a look at some other people's experiences of how their genders have shifted over time, or stayed stable, before we invite you to reflect on your own gender development.

Multiple experiences: Gender fixed and gender fluid

'It irritates me when people talk about the "gender journey". Definitely some people do have changes in their genders over time but mine has been pretty consistent. Let's not assume that the same thing is true for everyone. As a trans woman I've had far too much of people questioning my gender. I need you to respect that I've experienced, expressed, and identified my gender in basically the same ways for over 30 years now, and I really don't see that changing.'

'The biggest change in my gender had to be when I became a mother. The whole process of getting pregnant and giving birth tapped into something nurturing, feminine, and powerful for me. Prior to that I hadn't thought that much about gender, but afterwards I definitely strongly identified with being a woman.'

'I find it complicated thinking about the period of my life when I identified as a woman and tried to be super-feminine and desirable – during my teenage years and twenties. In some ways that was something that I was coerced into and I didn't feel it was "me". On the other hand, I don't want to buy into the misogynist idea that femininity is somehow more "fake" than masculinity. At the time I did enjoy being that girl and expressing my gender in that way. It also restricted me in many ways. When it became too restrictive, I became more butch, and eventually transmasculine.'

'Back when I was a boy in the 1950s, in quite an upper-class British household, the children were treated pretty similarly until they were ten years old or so. At that point, boys got shipped off to boarding school and girls didn't. At school it was like you had to go from being a boy to a man overnight. You couldn't show any emotion or you'd get ribbed terribly for being a weakling. Also for that period of my life I suppose I was bisexual because a lot of us did sexual stuff with each other, whereas during my adulthood I've very rarely had any sexual attraction to other men.'

'From a young age I found it exciting to dress up in my sisters' clothes when they were out of the house. It started as a thing I did because it felt mischievous: a naughty secret that I had. Later on it became sexual. For quite a while in my twenties it was a kink thing: whenever I did kinky sex, I'd dress in stylised PVC dresses, high-heels, make-up, and wig. In my thirties it shifted slightly again and I enjoyed sometimes wearing more everyday women's clothes and just being that side of myself around the house in a non-sexual way. In the rest of my life I was comfortable to be a man and to have a masculine appearance.'

Reflection point: Changing understandings of gender

How has your understanding of gender stayed the same, or changed over time? Have you always seen gender in the same way, or do you have different ideas about it now than you did as a kid or as a teenager?

How have your gender identities, expressions, roles, and experiences changed over time, or stayed the same? Think about early childhood, late childhood, your teenage years, and so on up to where you are now.

In Sub-section 3.4 we'll build on these reflections to think more about how you might tell, or re-tell, your own gender story.

3.4 TELLING YOUR GENDER STORY

In Section 2, we highlighted how gender has its own ever-changing history, a history that changes not just over time, but also across space. Similarly, your own gender has its own history. So far, we have looked at your gender history from the context you were born into, with all its intersections, to the changes that occurred while growing up. We want to take a moment to reflect on why we think it's important to know that there is indeed a wider history of gender, and that it's vital to know your own gender story.

Why is your gender story important?

The larger gender history is woven by many stories over time. Your story is part of it, and as such, essential. When we know our stories, we can become more conscious of the impact they have on us. We can also become more active co-creators in both our own individual story, and our collective stories. In many ways, we're always acting in the story of our life. The question is, are we also actively participating in writing the script, or are we just taking stage directions?

When we enact gender identities, expressions, and roles that are expected of us – and that may or may not fit – we're living a story that to a certain degree has already been written for us. Challenging those scripts can sometimes be impossible if we don't have the safety and support needed to break away. For example, many people stay in abusive relationships because they lack support, from both the dominant culture and their own networks, to move away from them safely. In Italy, the country where Alex was born, for example, divorce was not legal until 1971. This shaped the gender stories of many women who were legally unable to leave unhealthy relationships until then. A new societal story was needed to create safety and possibilities for these women, and it is still being collectively written.

This is why our gender story has power. It connects to the stories around us, large and small, and it connects us with something greater than our individual experiences and perspectives. At the same time, our individual experiences and perspectives weave the tapestry of the larger stories in a mutual relationship of expansion and co-creation. Telling your gender story may or may not be one of the reasons you picked up this book, but we believe it's crucial, and we'll come back to it a few times. For example, in Section 6, we'll talk about how increasing knowledge and understanding of our own stories can deepen our capacity for intimacy with others. This can improve all our relationships, from friendships to partnerships, and from parenting to collegial networks. Here are a few people sharing how knowing and telling their gender stories has impacted their lives.

Multiple experiences: Owning my gender story

'It was like never finding the right dress, that perfect fit. The words were always wrong, the relationships weird, for me and others too. It was like pulling on my own skin the whole time, trying to figure out if it was supposed to feel better. Surely at least it should feel more natural than this? Other people seemed to manage it alright. It wasn't until I understood that I was non-binary that things started to fall into place. Once I could tell people, "I am a non-binary trans masculine queer guy, who is into queer masculinities", life just got easier. Many of my gay male friends just breathed a sigh of relief. One of them said, "This makes so much more sense!" I couldn't agree more.'

'I was angry all the time. It's like I was invisible to any woman I ever fancied. Some of them broke my heart. They were my friends, and when I had gathered my courage and told them that I was attracted to them, they all looked away, mumbling something about how sweet I was, and that they didn't think of me that way. I wasn't sweet. I was a 30-year-old-man, still a virgin, with a high sex drive, who kept being told I was sweet, as if I were a child. Finally, I learned more about how dominant culture views people with disabilities. I came across the idea of disabled people being infantilised, de-sexualised, and sometimes almost seen as having no gender, especially no masculinity. That made so much sense! I had lived with cerebral palsy from birth, and from parents to school, friends to caregivers, it had been like the world had tried to build a brick wall between me and the idea that I could be sexual. I became more involved with the disability justice movement, and just stopped fancying non-disabled people who found me "sweet". Also, I am not a virgin any more, and my partner thinks I am a sweet man. That word "man", added after "sweet": That word makes all the difference in the world.'

'I just didn't know how to tell my parents. It wasn't just that I was a girl, when they had thought they were raising a boy. It was being a butch girl into girls. That part always stuck in my throat. Then I realised how many butch women of all sexualities and genders there were in our family. I just come from a long line of strong women! Once I got that, the words just started pouring out. It still wasn't easy for those around me, but I had a way of making sense of my story and my identity. I was just another strong woman in my family, that's all.'

ACTIVITY: YOUR GENDER RIVER

For this activity you will need some paper and a pencil or pen. You can also just think it through, but most people find it helpful to draw and write as they do it. First of all, take a moment to imagine your life as a river. Each bend in the river is a significant moment that led you to your understanding of your own gender today. Each bend is a person, event, book, film, song, encounter, object – anything really that significantly influenced your gender as it is today.

You can start at any point in your life but, given that we have focused on growing up in this section, we suggest starting from birth or your early memories. Draw your river slowly, annotating each bend with a few key words or images, to remind you what each bend represents. Your river can just be a line across the page or as rich a drawing as you want to make it. Don't overthink it. Once you've drawn your river, reflect on where you were in relationship to each bend. Were you in the river? If so, were you swimming comfortably? Were you on a boat? Were you struggling to keep afloat? Were you sitting by the edge watching your river flow by? Please remember to be gentle with yourself as you go through this activity, and take your time to breathe and take breaks as needed.

Some people prefer to use a different metaphor for this activity. For example, you might think of chapters in the book of your life, or levels in the computer game of your life. We'll revisit this activity towards the end of this book, so don't throw it away! Of course, you can draw as many rivers as you like. We find this activity changes every time we do it for ourselves! You might notice different things at different times in your life.

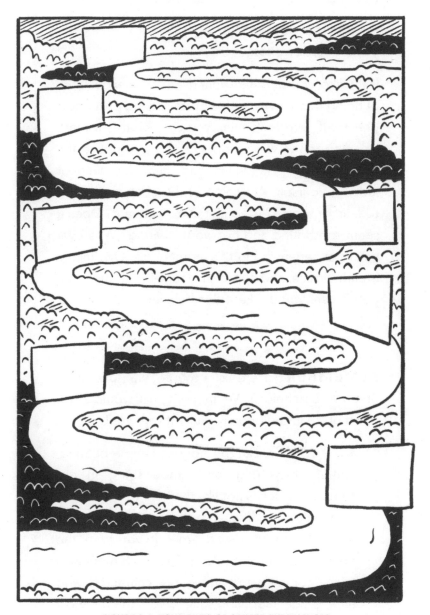

FIGURE 3.3: YOUR RIVER OF GENDER EXPERIENCES

Reflection point: Sharing your gender story

If you like, you can share your river, or the experience of doing this activity, with a trusted friend or support person. If you don't think you can, what is it that's standing in the way of doing so? Try to notice the obstacles with kindness and curiosity, without judging yourself. Are some of the obstacles linked to fear, or shame? Is your story too private? Does it seem too boring and not worth sharing? Whatever you're experiencing in this moment, it's OK. Take a breath, notice, and approach yourself with the same gentle care you'd take with a beloved.

REMEMBER: Here is a quote we love from Stephen Batchelor.[1] We thought this would be a good place in the book to share it with you!

So what are we but the story we keep repeating, editing, censoring, and embellishing in our heads? The self is not like the hero of a B-movie, who remains unaffected by the storms of passion and intrigue that swirl around him from the opening credits to the end. The self is more akin to the complex and ambiguous characters who emerge, develop, and suffer across the pages of

---

1   Batchelor, S. (1998) *Buddhism Without Beliefs: A Contemporary Guide to Awakening*. London: Penguin.

a novel. There is nothing thing-like about me at all. I am more like an unfolding narrative.

As we become aware of all this, we can begin to assume greater responsibility for the course of our lives... Instead of being bewitched by impressions, we start to create them. Instead of taking ourselves so seriously, we discover the playful irony of a story that has never been told in quite this way before.

FURTHER RESOURCES

You can read Jane Czyzselska's article 'Born this way' about intersex, including her thoughts on intergenerational trauma, here:

- — www.pressreader.com/uk/diva-uk/20160501/282312 499245079, accessed on 8 June 2017.

Harriet Lerner has written some brilliant books about how to communicate about difficult subjects in families, as well as a lot about gender dynamics, although with a fairly binary view of gender. Here is her website and a couple of books you might find useful:

- — www.harrietlerner.com
- — Lerner, H. (2001) *The Dance of Connection*. New York, NY: HarperCollins.
- — Lerner, H. (2003) *The Dance of Intimacy*. New York, NY: William Morrow Paperbacks.

You can read a bit more about narrative therapy, and writing your own life stories, in the following books:

- — Adams, K. (1990) *Journal to the Self*. New York, NY: Grand Central Publishing.
- — Denborough, D. (2014) *Retelling the Stories of Our Lives*. New York, NY: W.W. Norton & Company.

YOUR CURRENT EXPERIENCE OF GENDER

In Section 3, we explored your gender origin story: what gender context you came into at birth, your identities and experiences growing up, the intersections you experienced, and why it's important to know your gender story. Here in this section, we'll spend some time wandering in your current gender landscape. This is about where you are, right now, and deepening your understanding of your current gender location.

4.1 YOUR CURRENT GENDER

In Section 1 we spent some time breaking down different aspects of gender into identity, expression, role, and experiences, as well as explaining why and how gender is biopsychosocial. In Section 3 we explored where you've come from. Now, it's your opportunity to dwell on each aspect of your current gender in some detail. As usual, a little reminder to breathe, remain curious, try not to judge (if you can), and be gentle with yourself. Let's buckle up and take a ride around your gender neighbourhood!

Your current gender identity

As we mentioned earlier, gender identity is about an inner sense of who we are. If you feel that it's difficult for you to clearly describe your gender identity, maybe you have more than one. For example, your authors identify as both trans and non-binary. The whole point of figuring out where you are right now is to have some words that make sense to you when describing your identities. These words don't have to remain the same or be perfect.

Things you might like to explore here are:

- Which gender identity words resonate for you? You may want to revisit the various identity words we mentioned in Sub-section 1.1.

- If no words resonate, can you make up your own? Which gender identity words fit, and which don't? Do you need a combination of words you haven't come across yet?

- What words do other people use to describe your gender identity? You might even ask trusted people around you. Do they fit or not?

- Without overthinking it, if you needed to reply to the question 'What's your gender identity?', what would be the first words that came up for you?

Please remember that identifying as agender, or no gender, or finding the whole idea of identities doesn't fit for you, is perfectly OK.

Your current gender expressions

Gender expression is, as you may recall, how you express your gender outwards through clothes, hair, speech, and mannerisms. For example, Alex views their expression as masculine, with a touch of femme. Just as for identity, you don't need to choose an expression and stick with it. Many of us express our gender differently in various situations. Notice what your current choices are around the ways you express your gender right now.

It's important to take a moment to reflect on whether your current outwards expression matches your inner desires. Far too often, many of us adjust our gender expression to find safety, approval, or even just ease in navigating the world. There's nothing wrong with that! Going back to the example of Alex, he knows he would ideally express more of his femme side if people would not just mistake this for his identity. Are there aspects of your gender expression that you keep private because otherwise people make assumptions about you, judge you, or even threaten your safety? Are there places where you feel safe and comfortable expressing your gender exactly as you want to? Are there people who are supportive of your gender expression, just as it is? If not, we'll address finding community in Section 7. You don't have to take this gender journey alone.

Notice what your gender expression is in this very moment. If it feels right, that's great. If it doesn't, that's OK too. This moment is not forever, it's just a moment. You can change your gender story, if you need or want to.

Your current gender roles

Gender role is, as stated earlier, about the way we enact our gender in specific environments and in relation to others. You may already be thinking about your gender roles in relation to identities and expressions. Something that might be helpful here is to list all the roles in your life. For example, teacher, father, daughter, sibling, tenant, deacon, gardener, knitter, artist, rabbi, writer, and so on. Make as full a list as you can. You might want to think about how you spend your time, all the places you go to throughout the year, the people you spend time with, and how they see you.

Once you have your list of general roles, think about how your current gender manifests in each one of them. This might be the same, or different. Maybe you have a different way of thinking about each role than through the lens of gender; that's OK too. You might want to reflect on whether other people see those roles through a gender lens and, if so, how does that impact you currently?

Your current gender experiences

Thinking about the impact of other people viewing some of your roles through gender lenses takes us into the realm of your current experiences. How do you currently experience your gender? This is about the combination of identities, expressions, and roles, as well as your interactions with the broader world, and your other identities of course. Think about some of your most recent experiences, maybe over the past month or so. If you look at those experiences through the lens of gender, what do you notice?

You may want to think about navigating public spaces, such as transport, the street, shops, and so on. What are your current gender experiences there? Are they similar or different to your experiences in your private life, at home, and with your family, friends, and community? If so, what do you think is happening? Maybe your expression means that people who don't know you make assumptions that impact your gender experiences. This impact might be positive, negative, or neutral of course. For some trans people, for example, there may be a sense of peace in navigating spaces where they're seen as just another person, rather than as a 'trans' person. For others, this may not be possible, or desired, and there may be quite a lot of discomfort when navigating spaces where people don't know them and might make incorrect assumptions. Once again, there is no one way of experiencing gender, even when there may be similar identities, expressions, or roles. What are your gender experiences at this point in your life?

> **Reflection point: Your gender and those around you**
>
> Let's take another breath. That was a lot of thinking about the way things are. Notice what sensations, thoughts, and feelings might arise. If it feels tolerable, take a few moments to think about people around you. Who sees your gender the way you do? Is there someone in your life who 'gets' who you are, gender-wise? Is there someone who gets parts of it, but not others? If there are differences between how you experience your gender and how those around you think of your gender, what are those differences?

4.2 GENDER IN YOUR CURRENT INTERSECTIONS

In Sub-section 3.2 we talked about intersectionality as it applied to the context you came into when you were born, and when growing up. We've also discussed briefly where the idea of intersectionality comes from (reminder: Black feminism). Here we'll revisit intersectionality from the perspective of – you've guessed it – where you are right now.

FIGURE 4.1: INTERSECTION CROSSROADS

ACTIVITY: YOUR INTERSECTIONS NOW

Before we begin, you may like to go back to the map, diagram, or drawing that you created in Sub-section 3.2, when exploring intersectionality growing up. If you haven't done the activity, you may like to go back and do it now. It's OK if you don't want to – just focus on your current experiences and identities instead. If the whole idea of identity doesn't fit for you, it's OK just to read through, take whatever seems useful here, and leave the rest.

As you revisit your map, diagram, or drawing, notice what's similar and what's different in your web of intersectionality between now and then. Which things have changed and which have stayed the same?

Your current intersectional experiences of gender

As you reflect on your current identities and experiences, please remember that intersectionality is about the complex web that the interactions between different aspects of ourselves create. This is not an additive model, which means that it's not about figuring out how privileged or oppressed you are, either compared to your own self growing up, or compared to other people. This is not the Oppression Olympics of Gender! It's about appreciating your position in your own web, and in relationship to wider social, cultural, political, economic, and historical webs.

To consider where you are right now and to map your current web of intersections, you may like to consider the following:

- Where do you live right now? Is your main language, or languages, the one(s) of the dominant culture or not?

- Do you see your skin colour and tone reflected back in mass-media images? Did you learn about the history of your people in school growing up?

- Is your appearance, including your gender, seen as 'exotic' in the dominant culture where you are? Or does your appearance seem 'normal' where you live because you look like most of the people around you?

- Is your body considered normative, or does it differ from what dominant culture considers the norm because of its size, appearance, health status, disabilities, and so on?

- If you celebrate any religious holidays, are they the same ones when most schools and workplaces shut down or do they differ from official religious holidays?

- Are you safe expressing your sexuality as it is, or do you need to worry about other people judging you, being discriminated against, being arrested, or encountering violence?

- What is your financial capacity and class status? For example, is it similar or different to that of people portrayed in advertisements in mass media?

- Are you able to vote (if you are of an age where a person is allowed to vote where you live) or not? Do you have any rights under the law where you live?

You may already have considered all of these points in Section 3, when we first introduced intersectionality in more depth. If so, feel free to just focus on similarities and differences between now and your childhood. Below we'll revisit one of our own examples (Alex's) to give you a better idea of what we mean to achieve. Meg-John will revisit their own experiences as well, but in Sub-section 4.4.

Revisiting Alex's example and reflection

ALEX WRITES:

When looking at my reflections from Sub-section 3.2, I notice how much my comfort with my gender identity and expression has shifted. In some ways, I was more confident in my gender expressions when I was much younger, and I didn't fully grasp what was and wasn't socially acceptable. For example, I expressed my femme masculinity more fully. On the other hand, I am more confident in my gender identity now as a trans masculine person. Also, my class has changed as I went through several years of college, including being the first person in my family to ever get a PhD. My child is definitely growing up in a firmly middle-class family and has a different relationship to resources than I did.

I also realised that I was the first person assigned female at birth who moved out of my family's home without getting married first, or indeed following a man somewhere else. I emigrated by myself in my early twenties and partnered with people of different nationalities, something that my predecessors had not done. This has brought challenges of its own, in terms of being in a cross-cultural romantic and parenting partnership. I also realised that my immigrant experience is completely different from that of my great-uncles, as I already had a college degree when I moved – something I could achieve because of access to a free higher-education system.

Finally, although I had some serious health conditions at a young age, including a strep infection in my kidneys, I developed more impactful invisible disabilities linked to autoimmune issues in my twenties. My mental health status has also changed over time, as it does for many of us.

For example, I have acknowledged and learned about the impact of complex and developmental trauma as I have travelled on my own healing journey.

Here are a few more experiences from a range of people.

Multiple experiences: Gender at the intersections

'Growing up I just thought there was something wrong with me. For starters, I seemed to be a lot more scared than other people. I was super-anxious sometimes, and, apart from a few close people, didn't like others very much. I was also not very invested in pleasing other people, which girls my age seemed to want to do, or were expected to do. I fit in a little better with geeks and nerds, sometimes. I just thought I was super-weird as a child. Recently I found out I wasn't neurotypical – it wasn't a big surprise. I had found out bits and pieces about it over time, and eventually got assessed. Adults around me hadn't figured it out sooner because autism looks quite different in girls than in boys, apparently. Or maybe they just didn't expect a girl to be on the spectrum. Some of them just thought I was a spoiled brat. Now I can explain to people close to me what my needs are and how my brain works. I shifted parts of my identity from "weird girl" to "neurodivergent woman".'

'I am very active in fighting racism now and I identify as biracial. I wasn't allowed to do that growing up as I had been adopted by a White family and they just wanted me to act and be White, like them. Sometimes my identity creates conflict with my parents. I am a proud biracial trans activist. Not quite what they had expected or nurtured.'

'Nobody expected me to have divorce as part of my life experience growing up. But here I am, a divorced woman and a single parent. Sometimes it's hard, especially when I go to Church. It's like I failed in so many ways for them. I have to hold on to what I know to be true. I made the best choice for my child and me. If I had been a man, they would probably agree with me, but I'm not.'

'HIV positive is not an identity or experience that I had ever considered until I tested positive a couple of years ago. I was 17 years old. At first I was devastated. I wanted to keep it a secret. Other young gay men around me always joked about how tired they were of HIV education messages. Surely, by now, everyone knew they needed to use a condom, and only stupid people, sluts, and drug addicts got infected. I still heard those things after seroconverting. My stomach twisted every time. I just stayed quiet. Eventually, I found a support group for young gay men living with HIV. Listening to other people's stories was such a relief. I was able to start opening up about struggling with depression and meth use. I felt less alone. Now I am really open about it. I know what a big difference it made for me to know that I wasn't alone.'

Reflection point: Our changing web of identities

Our identities, expressions, roles, and experiences shift and change over time. Some change less than others, if at all. How do the things that shift and those that stay the same influence each other? Are there aspects of your identities that feel foundational to you, like a rock that supports you, no matter what? How comfortable are you with shifts and changes in your own identities, and in other people's identities?

4.3 GENDER BINARIES AND HOW YOU RELATE TO THEM

We've said quite a lot about the gender binary throughout this book: the ways in which dominant culture divides us into male and female bodies and then expects us to fit into stereotypically masculine or feminine boxes on the basis of that – and to be attracted to the 'opposite' gender.

To refresh your memory, we've seen that actually very few of us fit perfectly into those gender boxes, whether in terms of our bodies, brains, experiences, or expressions. Indeed, recent research suggests that at least a third of people report being in some way non-binary in their experiences, if not in their identities. And some linked research found that very few people have what used to be thought of as a completely 'male'- or 'female'-structured brain. Most of us have elements of both.

We could, perhaps, better view gender as a kind of spectrum between femininity and masculinity, rather than a binary where you are either one, or the other.

Femininity ————————————————— **Masculinity**

You might find it useful to think about where you would place yourself on this spectrum at the moment. However, you may already have noticed some issues with the spectrum idea. What is *meant* by masculinity and femininity here, given that they mean lots of different things? What if you move along the spectrum over time and in different situations? And doesn't a spectrum still suggest some kind of a binary, given that it is between two binary extremes? What about people who are beyond the binary? Hold onto your hat, we'll come back to all of these things in a moment!

Not the only gender binary

Before we get to that, it's worth pausing to reflect that male/ female, man/woman, and masculine/feminine are not the only binaries that we've come across in relation to gender. They're the ones that we often think of, but actually we've already mentioned quite a few other binaries over the course of the book.

One potential binary that we've touched on is whether a person is intersex or not. Again we've seen that our sex might be more accurately viewed as a spectrum, rather than an either/or binary, given that there's diversity at all levels of our biology (chromosomal make-up, circulating hormones, physical features, brain structure and chemistry, etc.). Also, some people who are not formally recognised as intersex may share experiences that are common amongst intersex people. For example, many people who are not regarded as being intersex have vaginas that struggle with any kind of penetration (sometimes called 'vaginismus'). They may have a similar experience to that of some intersex people who also find penetration impossible or difficult. Some people with small penises may share some of the stigma and shame that some intersex people with similar bodily appearances experience.

Similarly, the trans/cis binary is worth thinking critically about for a moment. We tend to define trans as shifting from the sex you were assigned at birth, and cis as remaining in the sex you were assigned at birth; but if we think of it more as a spectrum, that opens things up a bit. In some ways hardly any of us remain entirely in the sex we were assigned at birth, in the sense that very few of us stick with the set of assumptions that the people who were around us as we were born probably had about what a baby of our sex would do in their life. Gender politics has shifted so much during our lifetimes that most of us have deviated from the expectations that were present at the time of our birth.

Additionally, there are folks who have definitely shifted from the gender identity that would be assumed from the sex they were assigned at birth, and who would not necessarily identify as trans. Studies have found that a significant number of non-binary people don't feel comfortable identifying themselves as trans, perhaps due to transphobia in wider culture or because of an idea that being trans involves a more radical bodily change than the ones they have made. Also, many people who don't regard themselves as trans have a shared experience with trans people of being regularly misgendered and/or stigmatised because of their gender appearance. Common examples would be cis men who have gynecomastia (a swelling of the breasts) or cis women who have a lot of facial and body hair.

And then what about the binary that we've been drawing on throughout this book between binary and non-binary gendered people! Yes we know that thinking of binary/non-binary as a binary in itself is pretty full on, but it can be a useful practice. If at least a third of people have some non-binary element to their experience, then there are clearly folk who are on a spectrum from completely fitting binary understandings of gender to completely not fitting them. Also, many people – cis and trans alike – who identify as women or men do not actually buy the idea that gender is binary in general. It might be that they find those places comfortable enough to be themselves, but still see gender – more broadly – as non-binary. Or perhaps they would rather identify and express themselves in more non-binary ways, but that hasn't felt safe enough to do during their lives, or in their particular contexts.

Where might you be on these lines, if we saw all of these things as spectrums? We've added fixed/fluid as a further spectrum to the others we've discussed here. Remember how in Section 3 we saw that some people experience their gender as more stable, others as more changing over time?

Assigned female at birth	Assigned male at birth
Remained in sex assigned at birth	Shifted from sex assigned at birth
Binary in your gender	Non-binary in your gender
Fixed in your gender	Fluid in your gender

A bit of politics

There are political issues involved here of course, in relation to who gets to define themselves as intersex, non-intersex, trans, cis, binary, or non-binary. It would not be respectful of all of the people who have suffered greatly through being intersex, trans, or non-binary if a whole bunch of folk suddenly started claiming those identities when they have really never had to struggle in the ways those people have, living in such a binary, transphobic world. For example, we often meet cis men and women who, when asked to give their pronouns at the start of a workshop, will say something like 'him, her, they, whatever – call me what you like'. Of course, having, multiple pronouns that you use interchangeably can be totally valid. But we often get the sense that such folks are being a bit flippant, and haven't really thought what it's like to be out as somebody who challenges the gender binary with their very existence on an everyday basis.

On the other hand, politically, there can be something valuable about expanding the categories of something like trans, non-binary, or queer, until so many people fit under them that we're clearly talking about majorities rather than minorities. A lot of LGBT+ rights have been fought for, over the years, on the basis of being an oppressed minority that deserves equal rights. Some of that has been immensely helpful, of course. But there are limitations on what can be achieved if we present ourselves as a small group outside of the norm who are different in this one way but just as normal as everybody else is really. Sometimes it may be more radical to point out things like:

— Most people shift their gender over time.

— At least as many people have a non-binary experience as have a purely 'man' experience or a purely 'woman' experience.

— If you add together all of the people whose gender shifts over time or is somehow non-binary, who are attracted to the same gender or more than one gender at some point, who experience periods of no sexual desire (asexuality), who have some kinky fantasies or practices, and those whose relationships are non-monogamous some or all of the time, then suddenly cisgender, heterosexual, non-asexual, non-kinky, monogamous men and women are the ones who are pretty rare.

What would happen if everyone realised that they have a personal relationship with gender (and sexuality) so long as it exists in the world?

It's worth thinking a bit, yourself, about what it would open up or close down – both personally and politically – if you were to identify your sex, gender, and/or sexuality in the various different ways that we've covered here. We'll come back to community politics in Section 7.

Binaries or spectrums?

Let's unpack the gender binary a little more. Earlier we mentioned that you could view the masculinity/femininity binary as more of a spectrum. Here we want to suggest that it's actually multiple spectrums.

ACTIVITY: PLAYING WITH MULTIPLE SPECTRUMS OF GENDER AND SEXUALITY

Put a cross on the following spectrums for where you feel right now in relation to your gender and/or sexuality. Of course these are not the only possible options, so you can add more if you'd like to:

Woman ——————————————————— Man

Feminine ————————————————— Masculine

Gay ————————————————————— Straight

Femme ——————————————————— Butch

Soft ————————————————————— Hard

Submissive ————————————————— Dominant

Passive ———————————————————— Active

We hope this activity helps to demonstrate that our original feminine-to-masculine spectrum can actually be broken down into lots of different elements, depending on what we mean by it. For example, do we mean femininity as in being desirable to men, or being feminine in appearance, or being delicate and childlike, or concerned with others, or yielding?

Most people find that they're in different places on the different spectrums, not all down the left hand side or all down the right. For example, we authors both relate strongly to the identity of soft masculine: someone who is quite masculine in appearance and many aspects of expression, but is all about being gentle, kind, and/or nurturing. You might have noticed that coming across in our writing! We also have friends who are fabulously fierce femmes on the 'hard' end of the soft-to-hard spectrum. They love the femme appearance and express their femininity with dresses, make-up, accessories, dyed hair, and even glitter and sparkles, and they are also strong, powerful people who take no crap from anybody.

In lesbian communities there's long been a distinction between what people are 'on the streets' versus 'between the sheets', recognising that the toughest-seeming butch could well be a submissive puppy when it comes to their sexual practices.

It's important that we're not saying here that there's anything wrong with being able to locate yourself in a binary. All we're asking you to do is to notice those places where you might be more firmly at one end of the spectrum, the places where you might be somewhere more in-between, and the places where you might not fit on the spectrum at all. You might notice judgement coming up when you do this kind of activity, maybe thinking, 'I'm not enough this or that', or 'I'm too much this or that'. Just try to notice this, be curious about it, and treat yourself kindly.

Questioning the spectrums

Of course all of these spectrums have their limitations too. For example, the gay/straight spectrum suggests that there are people who fancy mostly folk of the same gender at one end, people who fancy mostly folk of 'the other' gender at the other end, with people who fancy each gender 50/50 being in the middle. But given that gender isn't binary, where is the space for people who fancy more than one gender on this spectrum? Or transamorous people who fancy trans folk particularly, or people who fancy non-binary people specifically? And what about people who fancy the same gender as themselves very highly, and people of another gender to them very highly too? Where does asexuality fit on this spectrum, or people whose sexuality is much more about the things they do with people than it is about what gender they are? We'll come back to such matters in Section 6, but this is just to point out that each of the spectrums could be questioned in this way.

Perhaps it comes back to Nat Titman's adaptation of a quote from the cult British TV show *Doctor Who*, which so many of us love, mentioned in gender warrior Kate Bornstein's magnificent *My Gender Workbook*: 'Gender is a big ball of wibbly-wobbly, gendery-blendery stuff.'[1]

---

1   Bornstein, K. (2013) *My New Gender Workbook: A Step-by-Step Guide to Achieving World Peace through Gender Anarchy and Sex Positivity*, p.xii. Abingdon: Routledge.

Reflection point: Moving around the spectrums over time

Going back to the spectrums you filled out before, you might find it useful to think about whether you'd fill them out differently in different contexts or relationships. If you like, you could even make crosses on them in different colours for different situations. You might want to think, for example, about where you'd fall on the spectrums when you are:

— out with your friends

— at work

— talking to a stranger in a shop

— dealing with professionals (doctors, lawyers, etc.)

— with your family

— in your faith/spiritual community if you have one.

Next we'll expand this idea to think about how you relate to gender in your wider world, in your communities, in your close relationships, and in your relationship with yourself.

Guess what? Yes, this is another slow-down and breathe page – you got it!

We know it may seem like those reminders are redundant, but we feel there's so much pressure to push through things in dominant culture, that we always find reminders to slow down and breathe useful. If you don't, feel free to skip them and move on. Remember, everything is an invitation in this book.

If you would like some reminders…

Take a moment to breathe. You don't need to change your breath in any way; just notice the air coming in and out of your nostrils and your mouth. If it's comfortable to do so, you may want to try breathing in through your nose and out of your mouth for a few breaths. You could also try breathing in and out of your nostrils. Whatever feels best.

If you're feeling that relaxing a little might be nice, you can try to make your exhale (breathing out) longer than your inhale (breathing in). How long you take is up to your lung capacity! For example, if when you breathe in you can easily count 1, 2, 3, when you breathe out you may want to try to count 1, 2, 3, 4, 5, 6. It's OK if that doesn't work for you. If it makes you more agitated, please stop immediately and just breathe as you would normally breathe.

Take as much time to just breathe as you want…

When you're ready to continue, we'll be here.

4.4 GENDER IN YOUR WIDER WORLD, INSTITUTIONS, RELATIONSHIPS, AND SELF

Before we move on to give some thought to how you might go about living your gender in your everyday world (Section 5), your relationships (Section 6), and your communities (Section 7), it's good to pause here and recap on where you've got to. Throughout Section 4 you've been thinking about where you're at in relation to your gender.

Now we're going to think about that in a slightly different way: consider the gender options that are available to you in your culture, your community, your relationships, and your own self, and where you're at in relation to these. Remember that we're thinking about your life as it is at the moment here, having focused on the past in Section 3.

Multiple levels of gendered experience

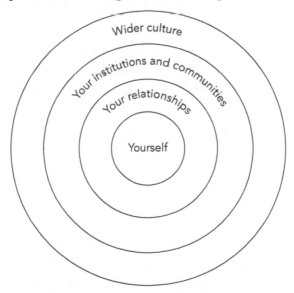

FIGURE 4.2: MULTIPLE LEVELS OF GENDER EXPERIENCES

As we go through the various levels here, you might like to make a note on the diagram (Figure 4.2) of any thoughts you have on the gender possibilities that are available to you at each level of your experience, and how you relate to them. Or you could copy the diagram into your journal and do it there, or just think about it. This is a little complicated, so you might want to read through the rest of this section first – to get a sense of it and to see Meg-John's own example – before coming back to complete the diagram.

Wider culture

We've already spent some time thinking about how dominant culture sees gender, and how the options for understanding, experiencing, and identifying our genders shift over time within that culture. An important further point about wider culture is that our current society, which is sometimes referred to with terms like 'consumer capitalism' and 'neoliberalism', encourages us to monitor and police ourselves in unprecedented ways.

Philosophers such as Michel Foucault have likened it to a 'panopticon' prison: the kind of prison where there's a tower in the middle and cells all around the outside, so a guard in the middle tower could see into any cell at any point. In a prison like this, prisoners begin to monitor their own behaviour because they know that they could be being watched at any time. Foucault says that our society is like that because we're constantly encouraged to scrutinise ourselves, compare ourselves to others, and improve ourselves. For example, adverts and magazines often sell the message that we're not good enough as we are and we need a different diet, clothes, lifestyle, or drug in order to be a better person. Social media often engages us in a process of comparing ourselves to everybody else, and feeling like we're not good enough. Encouraging us to spend all of our time looking inwards and scrutinising and judging ourselves is a pretty good way of both selling products and keeping us quiet, so that we don't make too much fuss about things that we might not be happy with in our wider culture.

Particularly, Foucault said that we're concerned with proving that we're normal, and policing our bodies and how they appear. So you can see how gender comes into it. We receive so many messages about what normal genders are like, and how our bodies should appear to conform to the 'ideal' image of often young, White, slim, non-disabled femininity and masculinity.

On the diagram you might like to jot down a few notes about the particular messages you receive about gender in your wider culture. Maybe think specifically about the media that you consume: the programmes you watch, magazines you read, music you listen to, social media you engage with, and so on. In what ways do those close down and/or open up your gender options?

Then think about how your experience of your gender fits within those options that are available. Which wider cultural messages about gender do you accept and which ones do you resist?

Your institutions and communities

At the next level in from our wider culture come the institutions and communities that we're part of. By 'institutions' we mean things like organisations that we work for, educational settings where we learn, prisons if we're incarcerated, care homes, and hospitals or clinics if we spend a lot of time in these. By 'communities' we're talking about the various groups and networks we're part of – for example, our faith or spiritual community, communities based on shared interests or leisure pursuits, the neighbourhood where we live, and the LGBT+ community if we're part of that (or sub-sets of this). You might find it useful to reflect for a moment on the institutions and communities that you're embedded in.

All institutions and communities have their own micro-cultures and these will also have their own ways of seeing gender. It may be that they follow wider society in their understandings and assumptions about gender, or that they say very little about it, or that they have alternative ideas about gender to those in the dominant culture.

Again on the diagram you might like to jot down a few notes about the messages you receive about gender in your various institutions and communities. In what ways do those close down and/or open up your gender options?

Then, again, think about how your experience of your gender does or doesn't fit within those options that are available. Which institutional and community messages about gender do you accept? Which do you resist?

Your relationships

We're going to spend some time reflecting on your intimate relationships in Section 6. For now, this next level in is about thinking through which are the most significant relationships in your life at the moment. These might be things like your friendship group, any partner or partners you have, your family, your closest work colleagues, the people you meet regularly online on social media or computer games, and so on. Basically we're talking about the people you spend time with on an everyday basis or feel closest to.

Again, we both give and receive a lot of messages about gender in the everyday babble of chat, gossip, support, and discussion that we have with our close people. As with institutions and communities, these messages might reproduce the assumptions about gender that are there in wider culture, or they might offer alternatives to these, or a bit of both.

Again on the diagram, you might like to jot down a few notes about the messages you receive about gender in your various significant relationships. In what ways do those close down and/or open up your gender options?

Then, again, think about how your experience of your gender does or doesn't fit within those options that are available. Which relationship messages about gender do you accept and which ones do you resist?

Yourself

Finally, we come back to you. There you are at the centre of the diagram, within those circles of wider culture, institutions, and communities, and personal relationships. The thought here is that all of the ideas, messages, and understandings of gender – or anything else – that we receive from those outer levels are filtered through our own mind, and then echo back up those levels as we co-create meanings with our friends, colleagues, and so on.

Some authors talk about it as like an internal conversation. The babble of thoughts that are constantly passing through our minds are the way that we internalise all of these gendered messages. They are how we do that self-monitoring that we're encouraged to do at the level of wider culture.

Again on the diagram you might like to jot down a few notes about the thoughts that you find yourself having about gender. Often these are quite judgemental and critical thoughts that flit through our minds as we go about our days. Some people use meditation or thought-records to slow down and notice them. In what ways do your internal conversations with yourself about gender close down and/or open up your gender options?

Then, again, think about how you'd like to relate to your internal gender thoughts. Which of the messages that you give yourself about your gender do you accept and which ones do you resist?

Revisiting experiences:
Meg-John's levels of gender

Here's an example of one of us – Meg-John – thinking through their own experiences at each level of gender. They've just given a few thoughts at each level, but there are plenty more they could have mentioned. Notice how gendered experiences echo across each of the levels, with all of them influencing the others. They're all interconnected.

MEG-JOHN ON WIDER CULTURE:

When I think about the gender understandings that are available to me in my wider culture, I'm aware of the way that ideas around gender are changing. For example, the increasing number of visibly non-binary people in mainstream media had a big impact on feeling that a non-binary identity and expression could be a 'livable life' for me. Specifically, I remember checking out the blog of the excellent musician and trans activist CN Lester a few years back and having an 'aha' moment that I could also use 'they' pronouns and adopt a non-binary identity.

However, of course, the wider culture I'm in is still very binary, and I notice that it's easy to feel invisible because of this. It'd be nice to see a non-binary character on the TV programmes I watch, for example, although it certainly helps to see trans characters in some of my favourite shows like *Sense8* and *Orange Is the New Black*, and I like taking on the kinds of geeky masculinity represented on *The Big Bang Theory*, even though none of those characters identify as non-binary. Of course none of these shows is unproblematic in their representations of gender, race, class, and so on.

MEG-JOHN ON INSTITUTIONS AND COMMUNITIES:

I'm lucky that the main institutions I'm part of enable me – just about – to live a non-binary life and to have this recognised. I can be out about being non-binary at work. Although I still get *she*'d by some colleagues who don't work with me closely or don't quite get it yet, my close colleagues have been brilliant. However, there's no bathroom for me at work, and my workplace doesn't allow me to register my gender as non-binary.

Another key institution to mention here is healthcare. I'm lucky to live in a time and place where non-binary gender is just beginning to be fully accepted and understood by gender services. So I was able to access top surgery (flattening of my chest) as a non-binary person, which has made a huge difference to my life.

Community-wise, I live in London, where there are several wonderful overlapping communities of LGBT+ therapists, queers, sex educators, and gender activists. The fact that on an everyday basis I can be around other non-binary people, and people who get it, makes a huge difference in terms of feeling comfortable and legitimate in my gender.

MEG-JOHN ON RELATIONSHIPS:

As I mentioned, most of my closest relationships are with people who 'get it'. One significant one for me, in relation to my gender, has been my relationship with my friend and colleague Dominic Davies, who set up Pink Therapy for LGBT+ people in the United Kingdom. When I changed my name, I was initially thinking that the 'John' part would just be a middle name, and people would still refer to me mainly as 'Meg'. But Dominic immediately started referring to me as Meg-John and I loved it and have used it ever since, along with 'MJ' for short. It showed me how relational these kinds of experiences can be. Sometimes you can't quite tell how a pronoun or name shift will feel until people start using it. I love that my name has been something that I've co-created with the important people in my life, from my parents through to current partners and friends.

It's also been useful for me to explicitly develop close friendships with other non-binary and trans people, like Alex. Spending time with my NB and trans buddies is so affirming and helps remind me that I'm not alone. However, it's also been equally important for me to develop friendships outside of queer and trans communities. Talking about my gender – and other things – with my monthly mindfulness group has been so important for me because they validate me as people who are outside of that world but who care about me and want to understand.

MEG-JOHN ON SELF:

My internal conversation about gender has definitely got kinder over time! Embracing a non-binary gender felt like an important way of saying to myself – and others – that my gender experience was valid, and wishing some kindness back to that kid who got bullied at school. Top surgery was so interesting from this point of view. I expected to feel more comfortable in my body post-surgery, but I hadn't expected the massive difference it made to my ability to treat myself kindly. Somehow giving myself that gift was a huge message that I was OK.

It's not all easy. Being non-binary at a point in time when it's still quite unfamiliar to people definitely leaves me questioning myself at times. And many of the role models out there are pretty young folk, so I can end up looking in the mirror wondering, 'Is this what a non-binary person can look like?' It feels exciting, though, to be part of this wave of people who are making sense of their genders in new ways, and I hope moving on the conversation at the levels of relationships, institutions and communities, and wider culture.

Reflection point: Kindness at every level

Picking up on these points about kindness, can you pause for a minute now to reflect kindly on each of the levels represented in our diagram? This time you might find it helpful to start in the centre and move outwards. Can you feel kindly towards the following?

— yourself, doing the best you can in the middle of a pretty complex and ever-changing gender landscape.

— the people in your life who are doing the same, even though they may make mistakes and not do it perfectly.

— the institutions and communities that you're part of, which may have become quite stuck, and struggle to shift with the times, and the people within them who may also feel stuck and defensive.

— the wider culture, which has come to this particular moment of allowing and enabling some kinds of gender shifts, while backlashing and restricting and restraining gender in other ways; and all of us within it who are finding it tough to make sense of gender in that context.

REMEMBER: Even when we identify, express, and experience our genders in very different ways, the gender struggle can be something that connects us. We're all struggling with many of the same assumptions and messages, and we all feel vulnerable about our gender in some ways. Perhaps we can endeavour to drop the specifics and to connect with each other kindly in this shared struggle?

FURTHER RESOURCES

If you're interested, you can read more about questioning binaries and identities in the following books (we'll say more about these in Section 5):

- Barker, M.-J. and Scheele, J. (2016) *Queer: A Graphic History*. London: Icon Books.

- Wilchins, R.A. (2004) *Queer Theory, Gender Theory: An Instant Primer*. New York, NY: Alyson Publications.

The amazing, wonderful Kate Bornstein's book that we mentioned is well worth getting hold of if you want to explore your gender in more depth as it has loads of helpful questionnaires and activities:

- Bornstein, K. (2013) *My New Gender Workbook: A Step-by-Step Guide to Achieving World Peace through Gender Anarchy and Sex Positivity*. Abingdon: Routledge.

Meg-John's original *Social Mindfulness* zine, where they explore the ideas of multiple levels of experience, can be downloaded from the resources page on their website, as can zines about how to do self-care and stay with your feelings:

- rewriting-the-rules.com/zines

IDENTIFYING AND LIVING YOUR GENDER

We hope that you now have a better sense of where you're currently located when it comes to gender, so let's move on to consider some more practical nuts and bolts. In this section we'll think some more about whether things are remaining the same for you or whether you want to make some changes. Because gender is biopsychosocial, it impacts so many parts of ourselves. This means that we'll explore changing – and staying the same – in relation to:

- gender identity

- the words you use for your name/s, pronouns, and descriptor/s

- body

- gender expression and roles.

5.1 IDENTIFYING OUR GENDER/S

You've already seen that there are many ways of identifying our gender to other people, from telling them what our gender is directly, or using gendered names or pronouns, to adopting – or refusing – gendered descriptors, such as 'Mr', 'Ms', or 'Mx', or 'Sir', or 'Madam'.

Let's step back for a moment to think about *why* we identify ourselves in these kinds of ways. What's so important about people knowing our gender? What does identifying strongly with a particular gender open up for us – in terms of our lives – and what does it close down? What about the idea that our gender is multiple rather than singular, as well as the idea that our gender is potentially shifting over time?

Why is this important?

So why do people find it important to identify their gender? Our view is that this is down to a combination of two things: first, the huge importance placed on gender in our wider culture (see Section 2), and second, the basic need that humans seem to have to be seen for who we are. Whether we locate it in our nervous system and/or in our existential longing for recognition, most of us seem to have a deep need for understanding, empathy, and validation from others. It feels wonderful when somebody 'gets it', or even better, 'gets us': seeing and acknowledging our gender as we experience it ourselves. It can feel very painful and uncomfortable when somebody misgenders us – for example, referring to a trans person as their sex assigned at birth, treating a tomboy as if she must really be a girly girl, or making an assumption that a gay man will be effeminate because of his sexuality. Being misgendered is not just something people can choose to feel OK about; it often cuts deep and goes right to our core.

This is why it's so important to check in with people about their own sense of gender, and to do our very best to refer to them in ways that affirm that. The language that we use for them – names, pronouns, descriptors, and so on – is one great way of doing this, as we'll see in Sub-section 5.2.

Gender identity

We've already said a lot about how you identify in terms of gender words (woman, non-binary, guy, tomboy, gender neutral, transfeminine, etc.). However, before moving on it's worth pausing for a moment to consider what identifying in such ways opens up, and what it closes down.

We mentioned queer theory briefly in Section 4. This is the academic area that builds on the work of people like Foucault – who we met there – criticising binary ways of understanding gender and sexuality. Another thing that queer theory does is to question the idea of identifying our gender, sexuality, and other aspects of ourselves. This might seem a bit strange given that we live in a world which is all about identity, and that we're very used to checking boxes on forms about our gender, race, ethnicity, sexuality, and so on. However, queer theory points out that we've only identified as individuals in these kinds of ways in quite recent times. For example, the idea of having a sexual identity (gay, bi, straight, etc.) was only invented just over a century ago. Before that, sexuality was more about the kinds of sex that you had than it was about you as an individual.

Foucault linked individual identities to the self-monitoring culture that we touched on in Section 4. If we have strong identities, then we also have a sense of what it means to be this or that kind of person, and we end up comparing ourselves to others in that category and policing ourselves to ensure that we're a normal, successful version of a person of that identity, whatever that might mean to us. Identity can also be a useful marketing tool in capitalist cultures – for example, selling people products on the basis of some ideal of what it is to be a teenage girl, a businessman, or a domestic goddess.

So we might question the idea of identifying strongly with any gender, given that this can be seen as part of a culture that's not very good for us. Queer theorists also argue that a gender identity often suggests that our gender is a fixed, unchanging, essential part of who we are, whereas – as we've seen – gender can be pretty fluid and certainly isn't determined by our biology.

What does identifying our gender close down? What does it open up?

Let's consider a few other issues around gender identity on a group level and then on an individual one. We've asked the question here of what gender identities close down and what they open up. This question is often a useful one to ask instead of a question like 'Are gender identities a good thing or a bad thing?' The 'close down/open up' question makes it clear that many things in life are positive in some ways and negative in others; they can both expand our possibilities and restrict them. It is less about right/wrong and good/ bad, and more about options and impact.

Thinking on the group level, gender theorists have highlighted ways in which identifying with a gender can close us down. For example, Black feminists such as Audre Lorde and bell hooks pointed out that second-wave feminists identifying strongly with the category 'woman', over all the other intersecting identities that people have, obscured the differences *between* women, such as the very different lives and needs of Black and White women. Second-wave feminists in the United States who focused on fighting for the rights of women to work outside the home frequently ignored the fact that most Black women had always had to do this, often working in the homes of White women! This not only erased the experiences of Black women, it implied that 'woman' was a universal category and experience, whereas many feminists were only talking about the experiences of certain women, usually White, cis, straight, middle class, and non-disabled.

Gender theorist Judith Butler has suggested that it can be more accurate to see gender as something that we *do* instead of something that we *are*. This is something we touched on in Sub-section 1.3, where we discussed how gender is biopsychosocial. Butler and others have also pointed out that identifying strongly with a category like man or woman, cis or trans, can reinforce the sense that these categories make sense and relate to essential, real differences between us, setting up an 'us and them' opposition that can easily lead to conflict. It also reinforces the idea of a binary, of course, leaving those who are somewhere outside the woman/man or trans/cis binary invisible and excluded.

However, also on a group level, scholars such as Gayatri Chakravorty Spivak have pointed out the importance of identity in battling for rights in a world which is very identity-based. Both feminism and LGBTQ+ rights have historically been fought for on the basis of people having oppressed and marginalised identities, and we now have increased gender and sexual equality in many areas. Spivak suggests that, for marginalised groups, it's often necessary to obscure the inevitable differences between us and to present a united front, in order to gain rights in a way that the wider world understands.

How about us, in our everyday lives? What does identifying with a particular gender identity close down and open up? You might consider that labelling your gender can feel like boxing yourself in, making it difficult for you to identify otherwise in the future, or to recognise that your gender might change over time, or to include multiple different elements – as we explored in Section 4. However, in a culture that does tend to identify people in relation to gender, endeavouring not to gender ourselves, and to go without gender labels entirely, can be a lonely and difficult path. Also, embracing a gender identity – even if it isn't necessarily forever – can help in ensuring that we're seen as we want to be seen by others. It can be a shortcut to explain some things about us. For others, having no labels can be liberating.

Multiple experiences: Claiming gender identities (or not)

'When I found out about transgender people, I thought, "That's me!" It was like a wave of relief washed over me. This made sense, I made sense.'

'I don't like gender labels; I just feel I never quite fit in them fully. Even the label "agender" doesn't fit me. Some days I feel like I have a gender, and others I don't. I guess I could say I am genderqueer or genderfluid, but sometimes the way I express myself stays the same for months. I just don't want to box myself in that way.'

'I am a Black woman. It's important for me to identify in this way. It makes me feel connected to the Black women who came before me and to all my sisters who share some of my experiences because of our race and gender. As a trans Black woman it also feels like an affirmation of belonging. I am a Black woman. There is power in saying that.'

Reflection point: Closing down and opening up

This is complex stuff, we know, but you might like to pause for a moment here, just to reflect on what has been closed down and what has been opened up for you by identifying as the gender you do (or don't) identify as, at this point in time.

Multiple gender identities?

Back in Section 4 we already began to unpack gender and to realise that there are actually multiple dimensions of gender, rather than just the one. You might remember the various spectrums we used to map the different aspects of our gender, and how we could be in different places on different spectrums, as well as in different situations and relationships. It can be useful to think of gender as plural rather than singular, as well as fluid rather than fixed. However, as with fluidity and fixity, it's important to remember that some people find their genders more plural, and others find them more singular.

Something that we've found really helpful in exploring our own genders is the metaphor of the 'community of selves' from the therapist Miller Mair.[1] This is the idea that we have multiple different sides to ourselves, rather than just one coherent self. Mair uses the analogy of the crew of a ship: all of the sides of us are on the ship of our overall self, but they may have quite different roles, or even be pulling in different directions. Different sides come to the fore on different occasions. You might have already noticed this in the activities and reflections throughout this book where we've invited you to consider your gender across time, relationships, and situations.

Our multiple selves can often be very gendered. For example, we may shut off parts of ourselves that are inconsistent with our birth-assigned sex, or which don't feel enough like a 'real' man, woman, or queer person. Others use their power and privilege to shut off aspects of ourselves as well. Consider messages like 'boys don't cry', or 'nice girls don't get angry', or uniform codes that insist that we always wear a suit or a gendered outfit at work. Such messages can either help or hinder us to express different sides of ourselves more freely.

It can be really helpful to think about giving all of the different sides of ourselves more of a voice, and making sure that they value each other. Therapists Mick Cooper and John Rowan (see Further Resources) talk about opening up the lines of communication between them. For example, Meg-John feels like they have gone through this process in relation to a masculine side of themselves, which they shut off when they learned at school that they couldn't be accepted unless they embraced a certain kind of femininity.

---

1   Mair, M. (2013) *Between Psychology and Psychotherapy: A Poetics of Experience*. London: Routledge.

They remember being drawn to a minor character from the TV show *Buffy the Vampire Slayer*, Jonathan Levinson. At first they thought they found the character attractive, but later they realised that it was more that they saw echoes of their own experience in this kid who was bullied at school and wanted to use a spell to make everybody like him. Embracing a more vulnerable masculine side has been an important stepping stone for Meg-John in finding a gender identity and expression that feels a good fit for them, and they're very grateful to Joss Whedon (writer) and Danny Strong (actor) for creating a character that's been so helpful! You might want to think more yourself about fictional characters you resonate with and what they mean to you in relation to gender.

ACTIVITY: COMMUNICATING BETWEEN OUR GENDERED SELVES

You might like to draw a picture of a boat and then sketch in some of your own *community of selves* as the crew. Where might they be on the boat? For example, taking the wheel, up in the crow's nest, captive in the hold, preparing the food in the mess, at the captain's table, singing on a stage, or walking the plank? Is your boat a cruise ship or a pirate's dream? You might like to give your different selves names, genders, and short descriptions. Think about who has bigger or smaller voices amongst the crew. Which characters can communicate easily with each other and which can't?

Alternatively, you could write or speak a conversation between two different sides of yourself. We'd suggest perhaps your inner critic and your capacity to be kind to yourself. Maybe you could create a conversation between those sides about your gender, as a written conversation, a spoken conversation where you switch chairs to be each side of you, or a comic with speech bubbles. We've included a couple of books with more guidance about exploring plural selves at the end of this section.

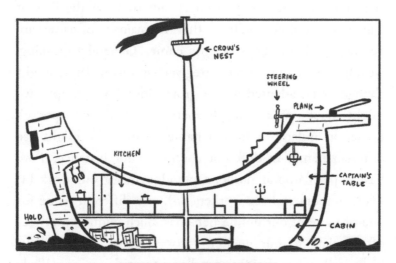

FIGURE 5.1: YOUR CREW OF SELVES

Keep in mind the plurality of gender that we've explored here when you explore Section 6. You may decide to use different names, pronouns, and titles in different contexts, for example. If you like, you could also think about how you can let other people know that you're doing this. For instance, you might do it through different gendered expressions, or by asking them to refer to you one way at home and another at work, or one way during sex and another the rest of the time.

5.2 GENDERED WORDS AND DESCRIPTORS

OK – let's get a bit more practical now. What are the other ways in which we can identify our gender to ourselves and to other people?

Names

One way is names. If you check out some of the lists of baby names online, you'll see that the majority of names are gendered either as boys' or girls' names. Generally speaking, we're given a name by our caregivers as a baby. These might change or be adapted as we grow older. For example, we might adopt a nickname, get married and take our spouse's name, or undergo a formal name change. We might use different names in different contexts – for instance, if we have a pet name at home, a pseudonym for our work (as many authors and sex workers do), or a different name for one or more of our online personas. Such naming practices often relate to our gender – for example, women have historically taken their husband's names, girls are more likely to be given feminised versions of boys' names (e.g. Georgina or Claudette), and many female authors have taken male or gender-neutral names in order to be taken seriously (from George Eliot to JK Rowling).

Changing your name is relatively easy in the United States and the United Kingdom. For example, Meg-John changed their name using 'statutory declaration', which just involves writing one sheet of paper outlining the change and having it signed by a magistrate. This piece of paper can then be sent to the passport office, driving licence department, bank, and so on to get names changed on all your documents.

Perhaps the more difficult aspect of name change is how others respond to it. Family members who had a role in choosing our name may find it difficult if we change it. If you want to, you might consider involving them in some way in the change. For example, Meg-John chose the name John partly because it had family resonances on both their mum's and dad's sides. Some younger trans people like to involve their parents and caregivers in choosing their name – for example, asking them what name they might have given them if their sex assigned at birth had been different. Some might even have a new naming ceremony with family, friends, and/or faith communities.

It can also take some time for people to pick up on a name change, so there'll often be a period when people use what is frequently called your 'dead name'. This can be painful for many people, and the supportive thing to do is to adopt somebody's new name as soon as they change it, but it can take a while, especially for old friends who are very used to your previous name. Some kindness and patience on all sides is a good plan.

It's also worth thinking carefully about the name you want to change to. It's fine to have more than one name change, of course, but that can end up being even more emotional work for you and for those around you. Also, if you want to very clearly signify a male or female gender, then choosing a more neutral name can make that harder. You might want to pick something very traditionally associated with men or women. On the other hand, you might deliberately want to have a more neutral name in which case a name that's used for more than one gender (e.g. Alex) or initials (e.g. MJ) can be a good way to go. It's really up to you.

Pronouns

Like names, there are various options with pronouns. Commonly used pronouns include 'he', 'she', and increasingly 'they' (see Section 1), but there are also many other gender neutral pronouns including 'ze', 'per', and 'hir' (you can easily find full lists of these online). Some people don't use pronouns at all but rather repeat names where a pronoun might otherwise go.

Some folks talk about people having 'preferred pronouns', but we've generally gone with 'correct pronouns' or simply 'pronouns' here, because 'preferred pronouns' can leave it open for people to keep using a pronoun that somebody isn't comfortable with, through the implication that their gender pronoun is simply a 'preference'.

You can stick with the pronoun that people have used for you throughout your life, or change from that, or use different pronouns at different times, or let people know that you're comfortable with either of two or three different possible pronouns. All of these options are OK. However, as with names, certain options will be easier for people in the wider world to get their heads around than others, so you may make a strategic decision to adopt a pronoun or pronouns that people are more likely to get right in everyday life, even if they aren't the ones that are the best fit for you. Changing multiple times can be disorienting for people too, although many do change a couple of times because it's often necessary to hear others using a pronoun for you in order to be sure that it feels like a good fit or not. It is OK to 'try pronouns on' and it can be useful to find a support group or friends who are happy to use different pronouns for you, at your request, while you figure it out.

You never have to share your pronouns unless you feel comfortable doing so. For example, if you decide to facilitate a workshop with a round of names and pronouns at the beginning, it is good practice to always leave open the consensual option for people to give their pronouns *or not*. Also, you might decide to correct people on your pronouns in some contexts, but not others. Meg-John has noticed that they rarely correct somebody if they introduce them at the start of a lecture using incorrect pronouns. That feels too exposing at the moment both for them and for the other person. However, if somebody uses the wrong pronoun in an email, they often use a line such as 'By the way, just so you're aware, I use "they" pronouns' in their response. They also have their pronouns in their email signature in order to reinforce the message with their correspondents.

If somebody in your life has changed pronoun then it's really affirming for them if you try to use it immediately, and stick to it as well as possible. If you're struggling to do this, then we find that talking about that person plenty when they're not around – using their correct pronoun – can be good practice. If you're unfamiliar with using gender-neutral pronouns, you might try practising them whenever you're referring to animals, because we rarely know exactly what sex an animal is anyway – for example, 'What a cute dog, what's their name?' or 'That bird looks like ze knows exactly where ze is going.'

Descriptors

Descriptors are things like titles or other words that may or may not gender us. Titles include options like 'Ms', 'Mrs', 'Dr', 'Mx', 'Mr', 'Miss', 'Lord', and so on. Other descriptor terms include the kinds of words that strangers might use for us in an everyday context such as 'Sir', 'Madam', 'mate', 'squire', 'love', 'pet', or 'babe'. In a group context they might include things like 'ladies', 'chaps', 'people', 'brethren', or 'boys and girls'. You'll have noticed that some of these terms are gendered and some are not.

We would love it if the world could move steadily towards more gender-neutral terms here – for example, moving away from the use of 'Sir' or 'Ma'm' in shops and restaurants and towards simply using people's names, or addressing them more informally without the gendered word: 'What would you like today?' is fine. If you often address bigger groups, you might think about moving from 'Hi gals' to 'Hi folks', or from 'Hi ladies and gentlemen' to 'Hi friends and colleagues'. People have different views on whether 'you guys' is a gender-neutral term. On the one hand, it is used so often for mixed-gender groups that it has shifted meaning over time. On the other hand, we might be cautious about whether it's another example of using a masculine term for people in general (like 'mankind'). Maybe check what people in your life think if you like using 'guys', or switch to a more gender-neutral term such as 'folks' or 'mates'.

We both think ourselves very fortunate to have been able to do a PhD at a fairly young age, meaning that we've had the privilege of accessing the gender-neutral title 'Dr' since being in our twenties. Obviously that opportunity is only available to a small number of people, and fortunately the gender-neutral title 'Mx' has come into use more in recent years. However, you may still find that you have to push some employers, banks, clinics, and so on to start providing it as an option on paperwork.

As with names and pronouns, decisions to ask for your correct title or other descriptor may change according to the situation, impacted by how safe or comfortable you feel on a certain day or with a certain person. We generally don't tend to correct baristas every time they 'Madam' us, but we might choose to have a conversation with somebody we're interacting with over a longer period – for example, the cafeteria staff at work or the manager of a hotel we were staying in for a week. We also want to be mindful of power and privilege dynamics and make sure we do not get people in service industries into trouble or jeopardise their jobs. With quite binary terms like 'Sir' and 'Madam', some non-binary people feel OK if they're getting some of each on a day-to-day basis. For example, Meg-John quite enjoys eating in restaurants where one of the waiters is 'Sir-ing' them and another is 'Madam-ing'. However, others may still find this misgendering difficult. We'll explore more about how you might express your gender in various ways in order to avoid misgendering in Sub-section 5.3, and then how you can let people know about your gender or correct terminology in Sub-section 5.4.

Reflection point: Ch-ch-changes

Where are you at with all of this? Have you made any changes over your life to your name, pronouns, or descriptions? Maybe you changed your name when you got married. Or you always use a nickname instead of your legal name. Or are you planning to make changes? If you have made changes in these areas, how have the experiences been for you? If not, what do you imagine these experiences are like for other people? Do you know anyone else who has made such changes? What have you done to facilitate and support those changes – or what might you do?

Of course the decisions that we're able to make in these areas are greatly impacted by the dynamics of privilege and oppression that we discussed in Section 3, and by the contexts that we're in. There's no one 'right' way to do it, and it's really important that we don't impose our way over other people's right to self-identify – for example, by insisting that they keep the name that we know them by, that they use 'they' rather than 'ze' pronouns because that's easier for us, or that they challenge people who misgender them even though we know they're not comfortable with that.

Let's now turn from identity to the options that are available to us in terms of our bodies, expressions, and roles.

5.3 GENDER AND BODIES

We've already discussed gender expression in general, so let's get into some detail here about choices that are available to you and to other people around embodied gender expressions. Because there's such a broad range of gender expressions, not all of them might make sense or appeal to you. That's absolutely fine. Remember the idea of gender liberation?

As far as we're concerned, it's really about people being able to express who they are and not having to fit into someone else's ideas of gender. What would it be like to live in a world where everyone can just be who they are, wear what they want, and interact with others in an authentic range of ways, rather than feeling constricted by gender scripts? We honestly don't know, but we'd love to find out!

Bodies in dominant culture and beyond

Dominant cultures in the United Kingdom and the United States seem to have a strange relationship with the idea of bodies. Since Descartes famously declared in 1637, 'I think, therefore I am', the idea of dualism, which proposes that our mind and body are separate, has taken deeper and deeper root in most Western European and Anglo-American societies. This means that in popular culture, our bodies are often portrayed as something to bend to the will of our minds, to be shaped to expectations of health, fitness, and standards of beauty that are imposed on us from dominant cultural expectations.

Gender has a large influence on these dominant cultural expectations. For example, ideas of gender in dominant culture might dictate how small or large our bodies 'should' be: how tall or short, muscular or curvy, and so on. Please note that we're not denying that many of us, including your authors, do experience a genuine sense of our bodies not matching our identities. What we're trying to highlight here is that we all have complex relationships with our bodies, which have been and are continuously shaped by wider cultural ideals. For example, Alex is an acceptable height in Southern Italy, regardless of how his gender is read by others, but in

Minnesota, where he lives, he is considered 'too short' when read as masculine and as someone living in White skin. This is because most White folks in Minnesota are from Germanic or Scandinavian descent and tend to be taller, on average, than Southern Italians. Similarly, the trope that 'boys don't have hips or butt' is mostly based on Anglo body norms. Expectations of how our bodies 'should' look in relation to gender are not separate from our cultural lens.

Before going into more details into expressions and roles, in Sub-section 5.4, we also want to highlight the fact that the idea that our bodies and mind are separate is just that: one idea. Many cultures and philosophies, such as Buddhism or that of the Sami people, view our mind and body as inextricably linked. This is also something that is starting to become more accepted in Western allopathic medicine, through advances in our understanding of interpersonal neurobiology. If you're interested in this topic, you may want to read books like *The Body Keeps the Score* or *When the Body Says No* (see Further Resources at the end of this section).

No matter what your identity is, in our experience, most people have complex relationships with their bodies. This means we also have complex (yes, we're using that word again!) relationships with our expressions and roles, as those are often manifested and enacted in an embodied way. This idea has also been described as 'embodied cognition'. That's the idea that our body and mind are in a symbiotic relationship. Our embodied experiences are inextricably linked to, and shaped by, how we think. You may have come across 'power poses', for example – the idea that taking and holding a particular pose with your body can influence your confidence.

Embodied cognition is very different from the idea of dualism, which proposes mind/body separation. To some extent, if we adopt this lens, we're saying that we cannot fully know how something will feel until we experience it. We can imagine it, talk through pros and cons, look at pictures, and process it through our prefrontal cortex, where our logical thinking happens – but we cannot fully know until we've had that experience. For example, we both had chest reconstruction surgery, which we thought through thoroughly, and discussed at length before undertaking it. However, we could not truly know how it would feel until after the surgery was complete and we could experience our bodies as they are now.

If this seems all a bit heady, don't worry: we're going to get more practical soon. We just wanted to set the scene first! By the way, if you don't see yourself as an embodied person, or as having a body, it's OK. Feel free to read on without buying into the idea of embodied cognition, and just focus on physical gender expression instead.

From euphoria to dysphoria and more...

Since we've already mentioned chest reconstruction surgery, often referred to as 'top surgery' by trans people, let's start from there. As well as dominant ideas of gender, we also have a sense of who we are. For some of us, that sense doesn't quite match how our bodies look and feel. This is not an issue only for trans people. If it were, there would be fewer plastic surgeons in the world, and they would not be as wealthy!

Many people have a lack of ease with their body as it is and might seek body modifications. These can range from tattoos and piercings to hormones, and from dieting and exercising to changing the size and appearance of breasts and chests, of hips and stomach, chins, noses, scars, and so on. If you think that body modification is just about vanity, let's think about the idea of embodied cognition again. For many people, experiencing changes in their bodies can actually significantly impact how they feel about themselves and their capacity for interacting with people around them. It can mean the difference, for example, between being an isolated recluse to becoming more fully involved with the world and other people. Let's look at this a little more closely.

Some of you may have experienced moments of pure joy, when you feel good about your body, how you feel in it, what you're wearing, and how you're perceived by others. These moments might be lasting, or fleeting and over in a few seconds. Those are moments of euphoria. We feel as if we're just who we're meant to be, fully ourselves. We feel as if we belong with ourselves and the world.

On the other hand, you may have experienced moments of feeling a complete lack of fit between your body and yourself, almost as if you and your body, or parts of it, are complete strangers to each other. These moments might also be lasting, or come and go in different situations, or at various times of the day. They can be moments of gender dissonance, sometimes also called 'dysphoria' by health professionals. Our bodies are not how they were meant to be; there is a disconnect. Some of you might also have experienced not perceiving yourself as others do. For example, you might feel enormous when people around you feel you are not, or you might feel revolted by parts of your body. These are also moments of dissonance between our bodies and how we perceive ourselves, also called 'dysmorphia' by health professionals.

In each moment there are so many more thoughts and feelings that we experience around how we are embodied and they can change dramatically over time. These feelings can be closely connected with gender in many ways. For example, they might be connected with dysphoria around our gender identities, that is, feeling that parts of us do not fit with who we are gender-wise. They can also be connected with our sense of gender expression, that is, feelings that parts of us do not fit with ideas of ourselves as masculine, feminine, butch, androgynous, femme, and so on. Because femininity is often devalued in dominant culture, this is an expression where many people might specifically experience deep discomfort, fear, and shame.

How we feel about our embodied selves might range from fleeting moments of unease to deep disconnect, where we feel it would be hard, and even impossible at times, to exist in our current manifestation. For some people, feelings of dysphoria, for example, might lead to suicidality, severe depression, social anxiety, and so on. Once again, these feelings are often talked about as being the domain of trans people. However, this is not necessarily so. While it is true that many trans people experience dysphoria, this is not true for every trans person. And many cis people experience just as deep a discomfort, fear, or shame around their embodied self as dominant trans narratives expect from trans people; cis women who struggle with the onset of their periods would be an obvious example. Another example is cis men who might have a smaller penis, and might perceive themselves to not be 'enough of a man' because of this. This example is, of course, deeply related to cisgenderism, that is, the idea that our bodies need to be a certain way to be 'normal'.

Expressing who we are in our entirety, including our bodies, is not something that's easily achieved since there can be many obstacles in our way. For example, we might need to access healthcare systems for some changes, and there might be a cost associated with this, or issues of prejudice and stigma to face. It might not be safe to express who we are where we live. It might also be too risky because of the ways in which our gender intersects with our race, ethnicity, disability, sexuality, and so on. In dominant culture, people do not have equal access to bodily autonomy, that is, the ability to make decisions about their own bodies, and any modifications they might like to make.

Making decisions around body modification

Body modification is not just about surgeries. We often change our bodies (through nutrition, exercise, tattooing, piercings, etc.). People have been doing all these things across time and space. None of these ideas are new to us, even though we're much more aware of them due to the rise of globalisation and the Internet. The reasons people have to seek body modifications are as varied as people's thoughts and feelings are. Nevertheless, there are things that people commonly consider when making such decisions.

Here are a few examples of issues you might want to think about when making decisions around body modification:

- What are the benefits of making this change? What are the risks? Do the benefits outweigh the risks?

- Do I have access to the resources, including financial resources, to make this change?

- How do I imagine I will feel after making this change?

- How will this change impact other aspects of my experiences and identities? For example, if relevant, how will this change my reproductive capacity, that is, the ability to have biological children? How will it affect the relationships around me, such as those with my family, my employer, my community, and so on?

- Do I have realistic expectations for this change? If so, what are they?

- What would this change open up, and what would it close down in my life?

- If I'm not able to make this change, what impact will this have on my life moving forward?

Other things that people often do before making body modifications is to carry out some research. You might want to talk to other people who have made similar changes, and also talk to whoever will oversee the change, whether it's a tattoo artist, prescribing physician, or surgeon. To a certain extent, it's hard to know how you'll actually feel about a change until it's done. The outcome might not match perfectly what you anticipated, for example. It is important to give yourself some room and support to adjust after undergoing any kind of body modification.

People around you might also have thoughts and feelings around those changes. Some of those might be helpful, others less so. We'll talk more about communicating with people around you in Section 6. First, let's look at some people's experiences around bodily changes.

Multiple experiences: Gender and body modification

'I had to fight pretty hard to have my tubes tied up at my age. I was in my early twenties when I started talking about it, and I was nearly 30 when I finally succeeded. Doctors, my family, and even some of my friends were really patronising. They kept telling me I was too young to know what I was doing; that when I got older I would regret it. I always knew I didn't want children. I didn't want to run the risk of getting accidentally pregnant and then dealing with that. I had to go from doctor to doctor, even see a psychiatrist, before finally being able to get what I wanted. When I did, it was such a relief! I am in my fifties now, and I am still happy with my decision, and proud of myself for fighting hard to have the right to control my own reproduction system!'

'I love my tattoos. They make me feel connected to other Latino men. As well as getting top surgery, getting the tattoos and piercings I wanted was an important part of expressing my masculinity. My family wasn't very happy with me. They said they made me look "bad", but I think they are afraid for my safety. You know, they think that other people will see me as trouble and start fights. They don't think I would be able to take care of myself because they still see me as a girl, rather than as the guy I am.'

'Getting testosterone levels up again in my body was essential for me. My sex drive had gone down in my sixties, and for me it was such an important part of who I am as a gay man that I couldn't stand it. Luckily my doctor figured it out. My hormones just needed a boost.'

'My face had severe scars from when I was 5 years old. I got burned pretty badly in a wood stove accident. I got used to it, even though people turned away when they looked at me. I felt handsome in other ways. However, I was kind of relieved when I could have plastic surgery as an adult. My confidence increased quite a bit, especially when interacting with strangers.'

'Getting genital surgery was essential for me. I couldn't shower, go to the bathroom, or get dressed without feeling overwhelmed with disgust and sadness. I just knew I couldn't live fully as a woman until I had a vagina. I know that many other trans girls think of their genitals in a different way and are happy with them. I just wasn't. I stopped going out, got really depressed, and found it impossible to create meaningful romantic relationships. Having genital surgery was hard. I had to jump through so many hoops. I had to get it together enough to convince all the professionals around me I could do it. The operation was challenging too and the recovery long. It was worth it – every minute of it, worth it. I needed it to be me.'

ACTIVITY: BODY MAPPING

For this you'll need some paper, a pen, and a pencil, and maybe the help of a friend if you decide to draw a life-sized body map. As you approach this activity, we hope you'll remember all our invitations to be curious, and be kind with yourself, trying not to judge. It can be difficult to treat our bodies with kindness because of all the negative messages in dominant culture. We hope you can get help from a trusted support person as needed.

Take a moment to draw a map of your body on a piece of paper, in your journal, or in a notebook. You could even get a larger piece of paper and ask someone else to trace the shape of your body around you as you lie on it. If those options don't feel comfortable, you can just use a 'gingerbread person' kind of shape.

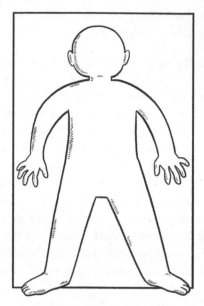

FIGURE 5.2: YOUR BODY MAP

Once you have a body shape, whichever you're using, start writing on it which areas you feel euphoric or dysphoric about, and anything in-between! Which areas of your body are you satisfied with, and which do you feel restless or uneasy about? Use words, colours, and shapes to indicate how you feel about the different areas of your body. You might even want to make more than one map to explore different feelings in different situations. For example, you might want a map for how you feel when you're by yourself, and another one for when you're with others, or even in more specific situations, such as 'at work' or 'during sex'. You can also annotate the map to indicate how your feelings change in different situations.

Reflection point: Considering your body map

Pause for a moment to take in your map. Are there changes you'd like to make on an embodied level? If so, what are they? Can you realistically make these changes? If so, what would some baby steps towards these changes be? If not, what are the obstacles? If you aren't able to make desired changes, what support do you need to live with your embodied self more peacefully and kindly, without making these changes?

If you think that body changes are extreme and not for you, please remember that our bodies are continuously being modified by the environment around us and by ageing. Our bones, skin, muscle tones, appearance, and so on change through time and space, even if we don't intentionally interfere at all. We don't look the same at 5 and 70 years old! All of our bodies shift and change as we go through life.

Well, that was a lot of words! It definitely seems like a good time for another break before continuing…

This time, we invite you to take a moment to notice your surroundings. Please use all senses available to you, and let yourself really take in where you are right now. Take all the time you need to do this – don't rush. It's OK to slow down…

As you notice your surroundings, you may want to take note of the following things, as you are able, and perhaps even name them out loud:

What are the colours and shapes around you?

What are the sounds around you?

What are the textures around you?

What can you smell in this moment?

What can you taste in this moment?

How many different things can you find for each sense available to you? Find as many as you can.

Then take a few breaths to notice sensations within you. If you can find a comfortable or pleasant sensation, stay with that for a little while. If you can't, you may like to shift your body, do something else, or bring up a pleasant memory to focus on for a few breaths.

When you feel comfortable and relaxed, or at least neutral, let's carry on…

5.4 EVERYDAY EXPRESSIONS

We've already talked about how gender doesn't have to be fixed or singular, and how it can be fluid or plural, as well as not a preferred lens at all on our experience. Next, we'll revisit some of those ideas in relation to everyday expressions. We addressed body modification in Sub-section 5.3, so here we'll mostly focus on other aspects of expression, such as appearance, clothing, movement, mannerisms, and taking up space.

Appearance

We modify our bodies on a daily basis as well as over longer periods of time. We make choices around hygiene, smells (e.g. perfumes and deodorants), make-up, hairstyles, and so on. These choices are often heavily gendered in dominant culture. Although there are generic products for everybody, such as shampoos, body lotions, and so on, many are divided into products for men and women. Sometimes products also target particular age groups, such as children and young people, or different race/ethnicities, such as in palettes for darker skins in make-up, and body lotions and hair products for Black people, generally women.

The way we make our choices around everyday appearance can be shaped by several cultural assumptions, including gender, but also by race and ethnicity, age, class, socioeconomic status, and religion. They can be influenced by our health or disabilities too – for example, how much energy we have on a given day, what caregiving support we have, or which prosthetics we have access to.

Dominant cultures usually have expectations around masculinity, femininity, androgyny, and so on. Sometimes these ideas might not be singular. For example, dominant cultures in the United States and the United Kingdom have oppressive expectations around Black women's hair, which is often represented as straightened in mass-media images of professional Black women. Black feminists have written about this topic in depth, and we include recommended reading in Further Resources at the end of this section.

Take a few moments to think about messages from the mass media where you live. What are the expectations for different genders, in relation to appearance? Do you fit with these expectations or not? If you don't, what is the impact of not fitting in with these expectations? Are there consequences for your sense of safety, wellbeing, which kind of jobs you can get, where you can shop, your health, and access to care?

If you do fit in with these expectations, what is the impact? What privilege might you benefit from that you maybe hadn't noticed before? For example, can you easily find make-up for your skin tone in a high street or mall store? Can you go to any hair salon or barber of your choice? Does your appearance reflect who you are or who others expect you to be? Whatever you notice, please try not to judge yourself. Rather be curious and compassionate, as much as you are able, in this moment.

Clothing and accessories

Another daily aspect of our appearance is clothes, including undergarments, and accessories such as shoes, belts, hats, and bags. These too are usually divided, organised, and policed according to the gender binary. As we mentioned earlier, expressions of femininity through clothing, accessories, and make-up are particularly heavily policed for all people, especially for femme-expressing people who were male-assigned at birth.

Clothing too intersects with many other aspects of our identities in both dominant culture and our individuality, such as age, race and ethnicity, sexuality, religion, and so on. Once again, you may want to take a few moments to notice what the dominant images in mass media are when it comes to clothing and accessories. Most major stores divide their clothes according to a gender binary of men and women, as well as by age. Some stores also seem to be clearly targeting specific class, racial, and ethnic demographics. Those messages around clothing and accessories are also reinforced by advertisements and popular culture such as pop music videos, TV shows, and films.

What we consider appropriate for different genders in terms of clothing and accessories has definitely changed over time, and it's different across the globe. For example, in Italy, it's not unusual for cis straight men to wear pastel-coloured shirts, including pink, something that might mark someone as not male and/or not straight in the United Kingdom or the United States. It's not that long ago that trousers were not considered appropriate for women in the United Kingdom and the United States. In some contexts, you might still see a clear distinction in clothing according to the gender binary. For example, it's still common to see female air stewards in skirts.

For many of us with gender expressions that do not fit dominant cultural expectations, this – together with appearance – is one of the most dangerous areas when negotiating public spaces. Clothing and accessories can quickly expose us as not fitting in, and it might mean becoming a target for public transphobia. Trans feminine people are often singled out for a specific form of public hate and humiliation (mentioned earlier) called 'trans misogyny'. When combined with racism and xenophobia, trans misogyny can even be deadly for many trans women.

Where are you at with clothing and accessories in your everyday life? Do you use different ones according to situations, such as at work versus at home, or with friends versus with family of origin? Do you feel able to dress as you want to, or do you feel the pressure to fit in with other people's expectations of you? Are there times when you might dress to fit in with specific gendered expectations? If so, what are they, and which possibilities open up and which close down when making those choices? Is it safe for you to dress as you want, or are there places, people, and situations where you need to be careful of your clothing and accessories choices? Once again, just take a few moments to notice, with kindness and as little judgement as you can muster, where you're at.

Movement, mannerisms, and voice

Other areas of gender expression, as pointed out earlier, are movement, mannerisms, and voice. Not all of them, or in fact any of them in some cases, may be fully under our control or conscious choice. These are often areas that develop over time, and which are again strongly shaped by gendered social and cultural expectations. These expectations also shift with age, class, race, ethnicity, disability, religion, sexuality, and so on.

These areas are often the main target of stereotypes in mass-media representations, and they can be very impactful. Children seem to pick up at a young age which movements, mannerisms, pitches and tones seem to be acceptable and which ones are not. These are also not universal. For example, one of us (Alex) noticed how in Italy and some other European countries, people assigned female at birth are not specifically expected to have a much higher pitch, whereas in the United Kingdom and the United States this seems 'natural', and White, middle-class women there generally tend to have higher voices.

People often think of voice, movements, and mannerisms as developing naturally, rather than being shaped by influences all around us. As we have discussed at length earlier in this book, gender is biopsychosocial and so are these traits of expression. They are also aspects of expression that might be heavily policed by parents, educators, partners, communities, and even strangers. People can be singled out by movements, mannerisms, and voice characteristics that do not fit in with dominant gender expectations. The risks this entails have already been pointed out earlier; and once again, feminine people of all genders often face the brunt of such policing.

We'll talk, in a moment, about negotiating public spaces, an area where such traits can make many of us particularly vulnerable. Before we do so, take a moment to think about your own movements, mannerisms, and your voice. How comfortable are you with each of them? How comfortable with these aspects of your gender expression are those around you? Sometimes people actively work on changing the way they move, their mannerisms, and how they speak. If you're interested in this, you may seek the support of peers or professionals (e.g. voice coaches or speech therapists).

Negotiating space while gendered

Many aspects discussed in this section impact how we negotiate space. We'll focus on negotiating space with those closest to us, such as family, friends, and partners, in Section 6. However, we'd like to spend a few moments discussing negotiating gender expression in public spaces. We've already used examples of negotiating pronoun use with people like baristas, in Sub-section 5.2. As we move through the world, we're constantly giving messages about our gender, whether we like it or not.

Our views of gender can be as sparkly as a beautiful rainbow unicorn on a bright snowy day, yet the reality of our options in public spaces rarely reflects such multifaceted beauty – it's much more drab. For example, we've already discussed the limited restroom options available in most public spaces. At times, we might need to use documents, such as driver licences, rail cards, bank cards, and so on, which have clear gender markers on them, which may or may not match who we are. This might lead us to feel more or less secure when negotiating everyday life.

The way we interact with the space around us is also not neutral. In the dominant cultures where we live, masculinity usually means feeling entitled to taking up more space. One example of this entitlement is manspreading (i.e. sitting with legs wide apart). There is no biological reason for manspreading. Everyone's genitals and thighs get equally uncomfortable and sticky on a hot day on public transport! Rather, this phenomenon is sociocultural and a byproduct of dominant ideas of gender. In a similar way, the dominant cultures where we live are plentiful in messages of 'stranger danger' for feminine people. These perpetuate the myth that women are at risk if left to roam the streets alone, especially at night, while masking the reality that most gender violence is perpetrated by partners, family members, or other people known to them.

Take a few moments to reflect on how you feel when negotiating public places, such as buses, trains, banks, post offices, government buildings, meeting spaces, places of worship, gyms, cinemas, shops, restaurants, and so on. Are there spaces where you feel safe, at ease, or comfortable? Are there spaces where you do not? Are there places you tend to avoid, or only go to with other people? Does this change during different times of the day? Can you go anywhere you want to, at any time? Once again, your experiences are not only shaped by your gender expressions but also by all other aspects of your identities, as we keep mentioning. Which intersections most impact your ability to negotiate public spaces with ease, comfort, and safety?

Some final thoughts

There is no one way of expressing gender, even within the same identity category. For example, for some people it's very important to be read in a specific way while going through their day, whereas for others, being read in a range of ways might not be impactful, or might even feel more affirming of their identities and expressions. Our ability to express our gender fully is also dependent on our socioeconomic status.

The choices we make about appearance, clothing, and accessories are often heavily dictated by financial access (i.e. how much disposable income, if any, we have), whether we are homeless or not, and whether we have control over our finances. Financial access also dictates how much choice we have when navigating public spaces. For example, can we afford to have our shopping delivered to our home, or do we even have a home address? Do we have to take public transport because we cannot afford to maintain a car or take a taxi? Whatever your choices, and those of the people around you, take a moment to appreciate all the various circumstances that might impact them.

Reflection point: Gender expression in our community of selves

If you like, revisit your community-of-selves activity, 'Communicating between our gendered selves', in Sub-section 5.1. Are there differences, in relation to gender expression, between the various selves you explored there? Take a few moments to consider any differences there might be in appearance, clothing, accessories, movements, mannerisms, and voice between different aspects of yourself. For example, is the voice of your inner critic similar or different to the voice of your creative self? As ever, this is just an opportunity to deepen your awareness and not to give yourself a hard time. Just notice, breathe, and stay curious and kind with yourself and others, as much as you can.

> **REMEMBER:** We've found it useful throughout this book to return to the idea of gender as a journey or as a work in progress. It's OK to take your time, to experiment, to try things on for size. We really hope that your own situation allows you to do that. In the next section we'll explore how you can go about navigating the ways in which your gender shifts or remains the same with other people in your life.

FURTHER RESOURCES

If you're interested in reading more about queer theory or identity, the books recommended at the end of Section 4 are a good place to start. We've also included a lot of autobiographical books and art projects at the end of Section 7 that can be really helpful to read when you're thinking about how you might identify and express your own gender.

Other books that can help you work through your own gender identity with lots of activities and reflections are:

- Hoffman-Fox, D. (2016) *You and Your Gender Identity: A Guide to Discovery.* Colorado Springs, CO: DHF Press.

- Testa, R.J., Coolhart, D. and Peta, J. (2015) *The Gender Quest Workbook: A Guide for Teens and Young Adults Exploring Gender Identity.* Oakland, CA: Instant Help.

A couple of great books on multiple selves, or sub-personalities, are:

- Rowan, J. (1989) *Subpersonalities: The People Inside Us.* London: Routledge.

— Stone, H. and Stone, S. (2011) *Embracing Our Selves: The Voice Dialogue Manual.* Novato, CA: New World Library.

Some books that are useful for thinking more about embodiment are:

— Hains, S. and Standing, S. (2015) *Pain Is Really Strange.* London: Jessica Kingsley Publishers.

— Hains, S. and Standing, S. (2015) *Trauma Is Really Strange.* London: Jessica Kingsley Publishers.

— Maté, G. (2011) *When the Body Says No.* London: Wiley.

— van der Kolk, B. (2015) *The Body Keeps the Score.* London: Penguin Books.

Here are a couple of books that discuss the issue of hair and Black women:

— Byrd, A. and Tharps, L. (2014) *Hair Story: Untangling the Roots of Black Hair in America.* New York, NY: St. Martin's Griffin.

— Prince, A. (2009) *The Politics of Women's Hair.* London: Insomniac Press.

The following is a selection of books by writers mentioned in the text:

— Butler, J. (2011) *Gender Trouble: Feminism and the Subversion of Identity.* London: Routledge.

— hooks, b. (2000) *Feminism is for Everybody: Passionate Politics.* London: Pluto Press.

— Lorde, A. (2012) *Sister Outsider: Essays and Speeches.* Berkeley, CA: Crossing Press.

— Rowan, J. and Cooper, M. (Eds) (1998) *The Plural Self: Multiplicity in Everyday Life.* London: Sage.

— Spivak, G.C. and Harasym, S. (1990) *The Post-colonial Critic: Interviews, Strategies, Dialogues.* London: Psychology Press.

GENDER, RELATIONSHIPS, AND SEXUALITY

You've seen now that our gender isn't isolated from the world around us, and that it's always in relationship with all other aspects of our identities and experiences due to being biopsychosocial. In this section we'll focus on relationships in particular. We'll start by addressing some of the issues and tensions around sharing our gender with others. Then we'll move on to discussing more intimate relationships, and how our gender relates to our sexuality and sexual practices.

Sharing any aspects of our gender with others can seem like a very vulnerable endeavour, and it often is. That's why we've dedicated a whole section to this topic! Remember to come back to your breath throughout this section if you're triggered, overwhelmed, or confused. We know we keep saying this, but it really is OK to take your time while reading this book.

6.1 SHARING YOUR GENDER WITH THOSE AROUND YOU

By now you hopefully have a sense of your gender identity, expression, roles, and experiences. You might also be better acquainted with your own gender history, as well as the location of your story in the larger landscape of gender. If you're not – or if you don't buy into the whole idea of gender at all – that's fine too. You can either keep reading, or go back to any of the other sections in the book, as many times as you like.

Let's assume, here in Sub-section 6.1, that you do have some sense of who you are, where you're coming from, and where you're located gender-wise. One of the things that might have come up for you by now is how you might communicate all the thoughts, feelings, and experiences with others. This can make you feel very vulnerable, and one of the risks of vulnerability is that it can be betrayed. Others might invalidate what we share with them, use it against us, or simply not appreciate it for the gift of trust that it is. Many of us have been hurt by others who have not validated and appreciated us for who we are. It's OK to think about who has earned your trust and who hasn't. As vulnerability researcher Brené Brown reminds us, not everyone has a right to your story. It is your story, including your gender story. Only you can decide who has earned the right and trust to know parts, or all, of it.

We'll talk about intimacy more in Sub-section 6.2, and how sharing aspects of ourselves with others can actually deepen our relationships. But here, we'll address issues of sharing aspects of our gender identity in different contexts.

Coming out/staying in

One of the common ideas about gender and sexuality in dominant culture is that of 'coming out'. This usually only applies to people whose identities and/or experiences do not fit in with dominant culture's normative identities and experiences. For example, when using this term, often people think of LGBTQ+ folks, and not of straight people. Most straight people don't have stories of gathering up their courage to tell their parents about their sexuality. Similarly, cis people don't usually have to share intimate details of their bodies, sex assigned at birth, and gender experiences with others, including colleagues and even strangers.

We've seen though that everyone has a gender story, which intersects with all other aspects of our identities, stories, and experiences. There's actually far more variation than dominant culture would have us believe. By now, you've probably caught on that this is a bit of a theme for us! Given the variety of genders in the world – a variety that goes beyond the simple binary of cis/trans – could we imagine a world where everyone, if they want to, gets to share who they are, regardless of their gender identity? For example, can we imagine a world where children grow up and decide for themselves what pronouns, clothing, accessories, and so on they want to use, or where nobody assumes a person's gender until they've actually disclosed it?

It might seem that we're light years away from that world some days! However, let's think about how our gender shifts and changes over time. Can you imagine a cis man in his late twenties needing to come out as having decided to remain a 'Peter Pan', gender-wise: that is, to not grow up and assume responsibilities that might be expected of him?

This might seem like a far-fetched example, yet ideas about responsibility, growing up, accountability, and so on are deeply connected to gender in dominant culture. These ideas of course also shift and change in time. We've witnessed the rise of the 'ladette', a whole genre of films celebrating the female equivalent of the 'bromance', and the laddish films of the 80s and 90s. So, why is it that some people are expected to come out about their gender, and others can cosily stay where they're at?

One issue lies with the whole concept of 'coming out'. What exactly are we coming out of and into? Are we coming out of normative and dominant cultures? If so, this would clearly delineate some identities and experiences as 'other' while reinforcing some as the norm. For example, expecting only trans people to come out reinforces the idea that cis people are 'normal'. Expecting only bisexual, queer, pan, lesbian, and gay people to come out reinforces straight people as the 'norm' of sexual identities.

Sometimes, when our gender is not quite in line with dominant culture's expectations of gender, we can feel a pressure to 'come out' from those around us. It can be hard to resist this pressure and to take time to reflect on who we want to share our gender with. We call this 'pressure', and similar pressures that marginalised people experience, 'enforced vulnerability'. This is a vulnerability that we're not freely and consensually embracing, but rather one that is being imposed on us by ideas of what is 'normal' in dominant culture.

Enforced vulnerability, passing, and pride

Enforced vulnerability, which includes pressure to buy into the idea of coming out, can become another form of oppression. Those who have normative identities already have the privilege of sharing only what they want of their identities and experiences. For them vulnerability is a choice that can be made from context to context (e.g. at work, home, with strangers, etc.). On the other hand, those of us who are seen as being 'outside' of the norm are often expected to be vulnerable about aspects of ourselves that are very personal, whether we like it or not. For example, virtually every trans person we know has been put in the awkward situation of discussing their restroom use and/or genitals with people who had not earned that degree of closeness, such as acquaintances, colleagues, or even strangers.

This, of course, is not a universal experience. Many people of all identities, including trans folks, can pass as fitting into dominant ideas of gender, whether they actually do or don't. Passing means that you're seen as belonging to a specific (usually dominant) cultural identity group, such as cis and/or straight people. When people pass, there can be a degree of safety, including not having to face enforced vulnerability. There's nothing wrong with passing and, in fact, it is a time-honoured survival strategy for many folks with marginalised identities across history. Passing can even be viewed as a form of resistance to enforced vulnerability, including the pressure to come out at all costs.

While there's nothing wrong with passing, it is not a strategy available to everyone. Another experience, which can also be seen as a form of resistance to enforced vulnerability, is that of Pride. When you think of Pride, parades might come to mind, or specific historical moments, such as the Stonewall riots, which were first and foremost about resistance against violent oppression. The latter are a good example, since they were led by many trans and bi women – especially Black and Latina trans women – such as Miss Major, Sylvia Rivera, and Brenda Howard. It is often people who are the most marginalised, and who might not have access to passing for a range of reasons, who adopt this other form of resistance to enforced vulnerability. Pride is about owning your identities and experiences openly, and often in community. In the face of a dominant culture dictating enforced vulnerability, Pride loudly declares that this is who we are, whether we fit into those expectations or not.

The idea of Pride is also not unproblematic. People often think of Pride, like coming out, as only pertaining to those who are outside cultural norms, in this case, in relation to gender and/or sexuality. Cis straight people do not need a parade, or Pride event, to generally feel safe walking down the street as they are, with their partners. This is of course a generalisation since there are many intersections of identities, and some of those, such as class, disability, race, ethnicity, or religion, might mean that it's far from safe for some cis straight people to be openly themselves on the street. For example, in recent years, we've witnessed the rise of Islamophobia, both in Europe and the United States, which has meant that it has not been safe for many Muslim people to be themselves on the streets, as acts of hate and violence have targeted them, just for who they are. Who gets to be themselves openly, who gets questioned about who they are, and who has to resort to passing just to survive – are, in fact, deeply connected to all aspects of power, oppression, and privilege in dominant culture.

Gender sharing: Some brief examples

Despite the risks that being ourselves openly might entail, and the pressure that we might or might not experience from the outside world, many of us feel a desire to share aspects of our gender with others. This makes sense since humans are indeed social animals. Here, we'll briefly look at a couple of examples of common social environments where we might want to share aspects of our gender with others. We've also talked about sharing our gender with others in other places in this book, such as negotiating public spaces in Section 5, and we'll address other relationships later in this section and in Section 7.

Family of origin

Our family of origin, that is, the people we've grown up with, might feel like one of the riskiest groups of people to share our genders with. They're often the people who've known us the longest and seen us go through the most. They might have their own ideas about who we are and have in fact often been involved in actively co-creating who we are by sharing their values with us (e.g. through parenting).

Not everyone chooses to share their gender identities, experiences, and expressions with their family of origin. For example, someone who enjoys a highly sexual expression of their gender through clothing and accessories in some aspects of their lives may not feel comfortable presenting in this way when visiting their parents. It's often expected by professionals that trans people come out to their family of origin to 'complete' their social transition, and sometimes this is even a condition that is required to be met before said health professionals 'authorise' treatments such as hormones or surgical body modifications.

This expectation is not only discriminatory, given that cis people are generally not expected to come out about their gender, but it can be downright dangerous if someone's safety, including their life and freedom, could be at risk when coming out to their family of origin. Can you imagine cis people in their twenties and thirties being expected to talk to their parents, or children, about their choice to take the pill to control their reproductive cycles before being 'allowed' to get their prescription?

Our families of origin do not automatically have the right to all aspects of our identities and experiences, including gender. Just like everyone else in our lives, we might have different degrees of closeness with different family members. We might want to evaluate whether our physical, emotional, and social safety will be at risk when sharing our genders with them. Here are a few examples of people reflecting on sharing their genders and gender experiences with their family of origin, or family members sharing their genders with them.

Multiple experiences: Sharing gender and gender experiences with family members

'My brother's wedding was approaching and I just couldn't bear having to wear a dress. I had to tell my family. My brother was very supportive, even though my mother freaked out quite a bit. We reached a compromise and decided to send a short announcement to close family and friends, asking them to not discuss my identity at the wedding, since this was a day for my brother and his husband. It worked out pretty well to share my butch identity in this way, in writing.'

'I chose not to tell my parents and siblings that I was having a radical preventative mastectomy. I am in my thirties and I feel that what I do with my body is really up to me. After losing both grandmothers and an older sibling to breast cancer, I felt pretty confident in my choice. However, I didn't want to trigger another family argument about cancer. I had my breasts removed, chest reconstructed, and only a couple of my close friends and partners knew.'

'My kid just sent me an email with some links to YouTube videos and a couple of websites saying, "I am trans". We didn't talk about it for a few months until we went to therapy. It was hard. I just didn't know what to say at the time. Now I wish I would have said, "Thank you for feeling you could trust me with this information. Is there anything you would like to change or do differently – for example, your clothes, hair, name or pronouns? It's also OK if you don't want to change anything right now. I am here for you; no matter what, I've got your back. Let me know what you want. I am so glad you could tell me. Thank you." But, you know, it's always easy with hindsight.'

'My mom just kept expecting me to bring home someone. When no girls ever came home with me, she started telling me it was OK to be gay, hoping I would still bring someone home. One day I got tired of all the indirect conversations, so I just sat her down and said, "I am pretty sure I am straight but yes, I am not a macho guy. I know I am soft and effeminate in the eyes of the world but that doesn't make me gay. I really just haven't figured it out yet. Also, I just haven't met anyone I like, that's all. When I do meet them, I will bring them home, OK?" I think she was confused even after I told her all that.'

Work

Work is another area where people might have expectations of who is 'required' to share aspects of their identities or not. For example, people with disabilities are often required to disclose their status in order to access legal protections and accommodations. At the same time, this disclosure might be detrimental to their work experiences, especially if their disability is stigmatised in dominant culture, as mental health difficulties and HIV status are, for example.

People with genders who do not fit into dominant expectations might be expected not only to be open about their genders at work, but also to conform to expectations around dress codes and appearance, whether those fit with their identities or not. Sometimes people are also asked to share their identities not only with colleagues but with clients too. For example, when one of us (Alex) was asked about their pronouns in a past employment situation, questions were focused on how he would 'come out' to clients. When Alex asked the cis person who brought the matter up to share how they disclosed their gender with their clients, they looked confused. However, both Alex and his colleagues were continuously presenting their own genders to clients. If you're curious on how Alex does deal with this, he simply says in the first session, 'My name is Alex and I use pronouns like "he" or "they".' Then he asks the client what their names and pronouns are.

It's up to you whether you want to be open about your gender identity at work, or anywhere. As ever, you may want to consider what this would open up, or close down, for you at this point in time. Here are a couple of examples of people sharing their genders and gender experiences at work.

Multiple experiences: Sharing gender-related information at work

'I am a very private person, so when I came back from parental leave it was hard to have to ask my boss to set up a lactation room. I can't believe I had to talk about what my body was doing and what I needed because of it. I was hoping they would have figured it out by the time I came back to work after giving birth! But no, I had to be like, "So, I need a lactation room. It needs to be lockable and it cannot be the toilet. Any questions?" I really wish I hadn't needed to advocate for myself in that way.'

'Being non-binary at work was tough. I asked people to use "they" pronouns for me, but then they kept expecting me to change other things, like clothes, or hair, or my name. When nothing else changed, I felt that some of my colleagues did not treat my gender identity and request for gender-neutral pronouns as seriously as they might have if I had been going from one end of the spectrum to the other. I started asking myself whether I really was trans and maybe it was too much of a bother to expect others to "accommodate me". Luckily I found a better job after a couple of years and now I am much more comfortable in my NB identity.'

'I was changing things slowly and gradually at work to start appearing more feminine. One day I got asked to set up a meeting with Human Resources. I thought I was going to get fired... But when I met with them, they asked me really thoughtful questions and said, "We don't want to make assumptions or pressure you, but your colleagues wondered if you were transitioning gender. If so, we want to be there for you and make sure you know we can set up trainings for your department if that would be helpful. What do you need?" I just started crying. I couldn't believe it. Maybe it was going to be OK to let people know I am a woman.'

Reflection point: Gender disclosure

Now let's think about your own life for a few moments. Are there any areas where you feel quite private about aspects of your gender identities, expressions, roles, and experiences? If so, what are those areas? Are there specific aspects of your gender that you feel particularly protective of? If so, what might be some reasons? If you're keeping aspects of your gender more private, what is the impact of not sharing those aspects with others? Remember, it's absolutely fine to keep aspects of your gender private and not share them with others. Here we're just inviting you to consider how you have made these choices, and how they might impact you.

6.2 INTIMACY

One of the reasons why we might feel a desire to share who we are with other people is because we feel close to them. 'Intimacy' is one of the words that are used to describe this sense of closeness with others. In dominant culture, intimacy is sometimes used as a code word for sex. You may think that people you're intimate with are those you have sex with. However, as we'll see, that's not necessarily the case.

Intimacy is a much broader concept than just sexual intercourse, although that is one of the word's meanings in English. Intimacy is about who we're close to, who we share experiences with, who we feel we can be ourselves around, and the sense of togetherness, ease, and familiarity this can engender. In many ways intimacy and vulnerability are close cousins. It's impossible to be intimate without taking some vulnerable risks by sharing a little of who we are with the other person.

At times there can be a sense of intimacy with strangers when we share meaningful experiences, for example, when sharing life or death situations, or intense religious experiences, or simply something like being at a large concert of a pop icon such as Beyoncé. All these experiences can be conducive to a sense of intimacy in large groups. However, such larger intimacy experiences are usually fleeting in their connection with strangers, even though they can last in our memories, or bond us closer with friends who shared them with us.

We'll talk more about intimacy with partners, friends, and those closest to us in Sub-section 6.3. For now, let's stay with this idea of intimacy a little longer. Because intimacy is closely related to vulnerability, it can also feel risky for a range of reasons. Often intimacy builds slowly over time as we figure out if we can trust other people. At times, our fear of intimacy and/or vulnerability can mean that we keep our defences up and refuse to let people in even after knowing them for some time. Alternatively, we can go the other way and flood others with our feelings, identities, and experiences right from the start, perhaps as a kind of test of whether they are 'worth' our trust and intimacy through putting everything on the table immediately.

There's no one way of doing intimacy and relationships. Sometimes the more risky intimacy moves pay off and lasting relationships are formed; at other times they can scare someone away. Sometimes we miss out on intimacy by being slow and cautious. Sometimes we take the risk but end up feeling betrayed or abandoned anyway. At other times the more gradual approach can be a safer way to build closeness. Intimacy can be viewed as an exchange of acts of trust, shared experiences, and commonalities, and the resulting build-up of many moments spent with others. Whichever way we build and experience it, intimacy has an impact on us and those around us.

Gender, vulnerability, and intimacy

Intimacy and vulnerability are deeply impacted by dominant cultural ideas of gender. Gender stereotypes often dictate how people manifest intimacy in their lives. For example, take a moment to consider who you felt closest to growing up. Did this shift over time? Do you remember whether your capacity to be open and honest about your thoughts and feelings changed over time while you were growing up? What contributed to making choices about opening up or closing down, in different situations, and with different people? What role did gender have in all of this?

Mass-media images in films, songs, advertisements, books, and so on often provide good examples of gender stereotypes, alerting us to how these may impact our ideas about vulnerability and intimacy. Such stereotypes shift over time of course, and according to the various intersections people inhabit. Some of the dominant images of gendered intimacy in US and UK cultures at the moment seem to be:

- intimacy mainly occurring in monogamous couples (usually of opposite genders)

– close groups of female friends sharing wine, chocolate, and talking about their relationships

– groups of men sharing beer, slaps on the shoulders, and high fives at sporting events, or occasionally being vulnerable with one or two best male friends about their feelings for someone of the opposite gender

– families of origin celebrating major holidays or life events.

Dominant culture has some clear assumptions about who we should be close to, share meaningful life experiences with, and find important. Those ideas are very gendered. However, intimacy is much more complex than that in most people's lives. In fact, intimacy is not a monolithic idea about closeness, but rather a large confluence of different types of togetherness that we might share with others around us.

Many types of intimacy

If intimacy is about who we share life with, and who we feel we can be fully ourselves and open with, then it makes sense that there are many types of intimacy that we can experience in our lifetimes. Here we'll give some examples, and then you can engage in an activity to explore your own intimacy needs, their priority in your life, and where they might be met or not, and by whom. Please note that this is not a definitive list. We're sure there are more types of intimacy that we haven't included here.

Many people experience intimacy with their colleagues at work. They might even have close colleagues who they refer to as their work partners or spouses. We often spend a significant amount of time at work and share experiences there, such as dealing with the same systems, people, and routines. All this can create a sense of familiarity and closeness with others. Of course there is plenty of work that happens in the home as well, such as cleaning, cooking, caregiving, and other house chores with those we live with.

Another type of intimacy is recreational or leisure intimacy. We might have passionate pursuits we share with others, such as book clubs, climbing, knitting, dancing, and so on. When sharing those pursuits with others, intimacy can emerge. We might also have people we share our ideas with and with whom we have a sort of philosophical or activist intimacy, based on shared views.

When experiencing things we find beautiful, we often want to share them with others – often, but not always, those we're close to. These can be experiences such as a sunset, or going to museums or art galleries. There is also a creative intimacy when we make things with others, such as writing a book or sharing time at a pottery studio. There are those we feel we can tell anything to and with whom we have communication intimacy, as well as those we can call when things get tough, sharing crisis intimacy. There are people in our life that we are committed to in a range of ways, and these could be colleagues, spouses, children, parents, and friends. There is also a spiritual intimacy we can share with others around our beliefs and experiences of faith or mystery.

All aspects of intimacy are influenced by our identities, experiences, and the culture we're immersed in. This is very evident for types of intimacy such as conflict intimacy. In Anglo-American contexts, for example, conflict intimacy can be frowned upon as alien and unfamiliar, given that there are dominant messages around conflict avoidance and the implicit superiority of 'rational' arguments and behaviours. Conflict intimacy is about those people who are worth our time and emotional labour, even when we face differences and difficulties between us: for example, when they might not be meeting our needs, or when we are hurt by them or they are hurt by us. Can we remain connected, even when in conflict, out of choice? If so, we're sharing conflict intimacy.

ACTIVITY: INTIMACY ASSESSMENT

Before we move on to looking at some of the most intimate relationships in your life, let's take a little time to go through an intimacy assessment to bring those ideas to life.

This assessment has been adapted by Alex, based on the intimacy categories discussed by Clinebell and Clinebell in 1970,[1] which were then adopted and used in a range of intimacy assessment tools by several people over the next couple of decades. It is the kind of tool that is often used in sex and relationship therapy, so you may already have come across different versions of it. Alex adapted a version that was being used at a clinic he used to work at, and that he believes had been developed by Michael E. Metz. Harley (1986)[2] has a similar questionnaire, so unfortunately the precise origin of the adapted questionnaire remains unclear. We hope

---

1   Clinebell, H.J. and Clinebell, C.H. (1970) *The Intimate Marriage*. New York: Harper and Row.

2   Harley, W.F. (1986) *Emotional Needs Questionnaire*. Minnesota: The Marriage Builders.

that what is offered here may be helpful to you. As you might have guessed from our writing so far, we believe that our intimacy needs can be met in varying degrees and by a range of people. This activity is an opportunity to reflect on your intimacy needs: where they are met, where they are not, and how important they are to you.

Directions: First of all, think about who meets the 12 aspects of intimacy listed below. This might involve one or more people for each aspect. Once you've done this, please indicate to which degree each of these aspects of intimacy is satisfied in your life. You can use a scale of 1 to 10, with 1 being 'not at all satisfied' (needs are not met) to 10 being 'completely satisfied' (all your needs in this aspect are met). Finally, rank each aspect in order of importance, with 1 being the most important and 12 the least important. Remember, there are no right or wrong answers. This is your own assessment and it reflects your own values, experiences, and needs. You're welcome to adapt it in whatever way works for you.

Types of intimacy	Who meets these needs	Current satisfaction	Rank of importance
Work Sharing tasks, supporting each other in various responsibilities (e.g. raising family, house chores, office tasks)			
Recreation Sharing experiences of play (e.g. fun activities, sports, hobbies)			
Mind Sharing the world of ideas (e.g. reading, discussing a film)			
Commitment Togetherness through dedication to common values/ideals (e.g. doing activism together)			
Delight Sharing experiences of beauty (e.g. nature, art, dance, theatre)			
Communication Being truthful and open with each other (e.g. giving constructive feedback)			

Emotion Sharing significant feelings (e.g. being vulnerable, emotionally open, and available)						
Creativity Helping others to grow and celebrating them as co-creators (e.g. nurturing self-development, celebrating change)						
Sexual Sharing sensual, physical, and sexual experiences (e.g. cuddling, kissing, having sex)						
Crisis Experiencing closeness through standing together at painful/difficult times (e.g. death of a loved one, illness)						
Conflict Facing differences, negotiating conflict resolution (e.g. arguing, disagreeing)						
Spirituality Sharing a sense of communion/belonging (e.g. philosophical or religious experiences, the meanings of life)						

> **Reflection point: Meeting your intimacy needs**
>
> Take a moment to think about where your intimacy needs might be met, and where they're not. How important are the needs that are not met, and those that are met? Does anything need to shift in your own life for your intimacy needs to be better met? Does gender have an impact on your intimacy needs? If so, how?

6.3 DIFFERENT KINDS OF RELATIONSHIPS

Having considered intimacy in your life in general, let's get more specific about your main close – or intimate – relationships.

It's important to remember here that the people who are closest to us are not necessarily our sexual and/or romantic partners. Some of us – asexual and aromantic folks – may not experience sexual and/or romantic attractions or relationships at all. Many more of us, although we do experience them, might not have a sexual and/or romantic partner at this point in time. Most of us will have phases of our lives when we don't. Among those of us who do have a partner or partners, the people we have sex with may not be the ones we feel romantically involved with. These things can be found in different places as well as in the same place. And even when we have one or more partners who we're both sexually and romantically attracted to, we may well get many – or even most – of our intimacy needs and desires met in other relationships.

Meg-John has written elsewhere – in their book *Rewriting the Rules* about the issues with the dominant cultural expectation – that we'll look for all our needs and desires to be met in one person or relationship. It puts a lot of pressure on ourselves and the other person if we expect the same relationship to fulfil all of our desires: for example, if we expect the same person to be our best friend, hot lover, co-parent, trusted confidante, everyday co-habitor, and cheerleader. It's a lot to expect somebody to share all of our values, to challenge us to think differently about things, to validate us as we are, to give us a sense of belonging and safety, and to encourage us into new adventures and ways of being. You might have noticed that many of these things that we might want are actually quite contradictory and rather difficult, therefore, to find in just one person.

Your close relationships

So let's think about your intimate relationships, remembering to be open to considering relationships of all kinds: old and new friends, partners, colleagues, lovers, family members, neighbours, friends-with-benefits, people in your community, even companion animals. Some people like to include their relationships with whole groups of people here, or people whom they relate to who don't reciprocate (like a favourite author, presenter, or fictional character). Others even include the places that mean a lot to them, or their relationships with valued objects like a soft toy, a particular tree, or the planet as a whole.

ACTIVITY: YOUR CIRCLES OF INTIMACY

Thinking back to the intimacy assessment that you explored earlier, who (or what) are your closest people (or other beings)? You might like to list them as they come to mind, or perhaps to write them into something like the diagram below (Figure 6.1), with yourself in the middle, your most intimate relationships at the next level out, then the other relationships you have close contact with but which are perhaps not quite as intimate, and finally the relationships in your life you wouldn't describe as that close or intimate.

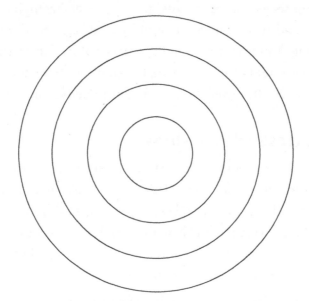

FIGURE 6.1: CONCENTRIC CIRCLES OF CLOSENESS

Notice how you've decided who to include as more or less intimate here. What was your basis for making those choices? For example, it might be one or more of the following:

- the person/people you spend most time with on an everyday basis

- the person/people you could call at 3am if you were having a crisis

- the person/people you feel most able to be vulnerable around

- the person/people you've known the longest

- the person/people you have sexy, romantic, or fond feelings for

- the person/people you feel know you the best

- some other criteria.

You might also like to start to think about the place of gender in all of this. Do your own gender and/or the gender of others impact on who your most intimate people are?

Partner relationships and gender

Let's focus on sexual, partner, and/or romantic relationships for a moment, if these things are something that you have in your life. Of course the template for 'good', 'successful', or 'ideal' relationships that we see reflected most often in wider society is heavily gendered: one man and one woman in a romantic, sexual, monogamous, coupled partnership. Indeed there are whole bestselling self-help book series written on the premise that relationships will always involve one man and one woman, and that most of the difficulties that people have in those relationships are down to gender.

Many mainstream women's and men's magazines make the same assumption. Our therapeutic work with 'same-gender' couples suggests that it's certainly not that simple! However, gendered expectations can and do put some man/woman relationships under strain.

Also the 'relationship escalator' (i.e. the idea of a linear trajectory of progress in relationships that people are culturally encouraged to follow) is pretty gendered, as there are gender assumptions at each stage. Take the following examples: Who is meant to ask who out on a date, initiate sex, and say 'I love you' first? Who is meant to bring in most money, pay the rent/mortgage? Who is meant to do the most emotional labour? There is also the fact that it's assumed the partners will get married and have kids on the escalator – two practices that have traditionally been highly gendered although this is slowly shifting with increasing recognition of 'same-gender' partnerships and diverse forms of parenting.

Actually, of course, there are many ways of doing relationships, and the part gender may play can be anything: from a vital role to having very little impact at all, and everything in-between. By now you will probably not be surprised that this is our view!

It's impossible to go into all of the various possible relationships structures, but below is a list of some of the models of relationships that currently exist in our culture. You might like to do some research on any that are unfamiliar to you, and we've included some more books and websites about them in Further Resources at the end of this section. We've also linked to a zine which helps you to create your own relationship user guide, in case you're interested in doing some more in-depth exploration into your preferred ways of doing relationships and how you might communicate about these with others.

Lots of relationship models

Monogamous, polyamorous, polygyny, celibate, mono-gamish, solo poly, fuckbuddies, hierarchical poly, bromantic, poly family, hook-up, single, polygamous, primary/secon-dary, singlish, line marriage, new monogamy, mono/poly, swinging, polyandry, open relationship, egalitarian poly, polycule, friends-with-benefits arrangement, poly-fidelitous, plural marriage, relationship anarchy.

Escaping gender is probably impossible

Of course, even in relationship forms that differ from the dominant cultural form of monogamous 'opposite-gender' coupledom, gender dynamics often still come into it, however much we may wish to escape from them. For example, women in polyamorous set-ups can still find themselves taking on conventional roles in terms of child-rearing or emotional labour. People in 'same-gender' relationships can sometimes find their relationships dividing along more conventionally gendered lines, with one person doing more of the conventionally 'male' roles and the other the more conventionally 'female' ones. Of course this isn't always the case, and other people find that polyamorous or 'same-gender' relationships liberate them from many of the expectations around gender. It's just important to remember that in a highly gendered world it rarely disappears entirely.

Let's now look at some people's experience of the ways in which gender plays out in their sexual, romantic, and partner relationships.

Multiple experiences: Being my gender in my relationships

'When I got together with my partner, I had several male and female friends. I've noticed that, while my female friendships have remained close, my male friendships have mostly dropped away. He never explicitly said that he was uncomfortable with me being close to other guys, but that's definitely the impression I got. I really miss a couple of those friendships because they were the oldest ones that I had.'

'Gender was a huge issue in my relationships during my transition. I was married with a wife and she was *not* comfortable with me being a woman. We had some couple therapy, but it often felt – even there – that being trans was somehow a problem that I should fix so that it went away. Eventually I found a trans-affirmative therapist and navigated leaving that relationship as my transition continued. Fortunately my kids have been a lot more accepting of their mom – as they now call me. These days I'm in a relationship with a wonderful woman, and very proud to finally be what I always felt I was: a lesbian. My ex-wife and I are friends now and I am grateful we could change our relationship that way. We have been in each other's lives for a long time and we're still co-parents.'

'Definitely the closest people in my life are women – or should I say "not men"? – because I am close with a couple of non-binary folks. I seek out women's and femme spaces, and my poly partners are all women/femmes or people who are closely allied with women's experience. I couldn't really imagine it otherwise. I love my femmes!'

'I love being solo-poly because it means that my primary relationship is with myself. I make sure I get plenty of time for solitude and for reflecting on myself and my relationships with others. I have several important people in my life, some of whom I have a sexual connection with, some romantic, and some neither. We're all aware that those things can change over time too. As a non-binary person I notice how those different relationships bring out differently gendered sides of me. I'm a butch bottom with one lover, a nurturing top with another. I love blokey drinks with one of my mates, and feeling quite precious in a feminine way with another one. I'm so happy to have found a relationship style that suits me so well.'

'As a survivor of abuse, I'm definitely wary of relationships with men, even though I'm a man myself. It's something I'm still working on, but until I have, I'm far more comfortable with the main people in my life being women.'

When it comes to gender and close relationships, it's important also to reflect on the role that other people have in your gender, and vice versa. As some of these examples demonstrate, the relationships in our lives can be very powerful in restricting, or expanding, our gender options. For example, in the United Kingdom legally there is still a 'spousal veto' in place, which means that a spouse can refuse a trans partner getting a gender recognition certificate. Pressures to remain married, or not get divorced, have played a large part in many trans people waiting longer than they might otherwise have done to embark on a process that feels important – or even life-saving – for them. On the flip side, having sides of ourselves recognised in relationships can be the first trigger to a realisation that perhaps our gender isn't as we previously thought. Friends, partners, and lovers can bring out aspects of us that we hadn't even realised were there, and it can be amazing – if sometimes rather terrifying – if we then have those sides validated and affirmed by them.

While it's important to recognise that our gender can have an impact on the people in our lives, it's never OK for somebody else to determine how you can or can't identify or express yourself, or to have control over your body. This is a form of emotional abuse, and we've included some materials in Further Resources at the end of this section about how to recognise this and where you can look for help if it does happen to you.

However, if we are making changes, we do need to be mindful of their potential impact on other people, giving them time to process this, and to make any changes that they may need to make around it. For example, it may not be easy for somebody who has always identified strongly with being a lesbian to find themselves with a male partner, or for a parent to shift from speaking about their son to speaking about their offspring, or for a monogamous person to move to a more open relationship in order to allow their partner to experience and express different sides of their gender in a sexual context. Sometimes relationships may have to change radically, or even end, under these circumstances. At other times we may be surprised at how other people respond, and even embrace such changes, perhaps discovering previously untapped sides of themselves in the process.

In Section 7 we'll focus in even more detail on our sexuality, sexual relationships, and sexual practices, again remembering that – like romantic relationships or partnerships – these are not a feature of everybody's lives.

Reflection point: How you do relationships

What's your current way of doing relationships and how does it work for your gender? Remembering back to the community of selves that we covered in Section 5, you might like to think about which parts of your own community get expressed, and in which relationships, as well as which selves don't get expressed, or are given less room.

6.4 SEXUALITY AND SEXUAL PRACTICES

When it comes to sexuality and sexual practices, there are even more gendered assumptions than there are for relationships more broadly. You saw earlier in this book how the idea of sexuality in our culture is intrinsically bound up with assumptions about gender and genitals. The dominant cultural norms of gender, sexuality, and sex look something like this:

- You have a body that was born male (with a penis) or female (with a vagina).

- This means that you become either a masculine man or feminine woman.

- Part of this masculinity or femininity is to be attracted to, and desired by, the 'opposite' gender.

- You demonstrate this desire through sex, which is generally assumed to involve a penis going into a vagina (PIV sex).

Through reading this book we hope you've come to realise that these first two points are both questionable, as is the idea that one follows on from the other. Here we also want to briefly problematise the latter two points. For more evidence about why they are problematic, and ideas about how you might do things differently, you may want to check out a couple of Meg-John's other books about sex and sexuality listed in Further Resources at the end of this section. In the rest of this section we'll explore the diversity of ways in which people's sexuality and sexual practices can be connected – or not – to their gender.

Gendered assumptions about sexuality and sex

One way in which our gender and sexuality tend to be connected in wider culture is in the idea that people have a 'sexual orientation' that is defined by their gender and the gender of the people they're attracted to. To this day this is often understood as binary: you're gay or you're straight. When we considered dimensions in Sub-section 4.3, we mentioned that this can be usefully regarded as more of a spectrum. Recent research has found that, if we do that, nearly half of young people put themselves somewhere in-between totally gay and totally straight.

We also saw in Sub-section 4.3 that, given that gender itself isn't binary, sexual orientation can't actually be mapped onto a spectrum like this. Lots of people are attracted to more than one gender (the most common definition of bisexuality in bi communities), or to people regardless of their gender (some people's definition of pansexual, bisexual, or queer), or specifically to genders beyond men and women. There are also many people who don't experience sexual attraction at all (asexual or ace), or only sometimes or in specific situations (grey-A or demisexual). And there are lots of people for whom the main features of sexuality are not about the gender of the people they're attracted to, but rather about playing certain roles, experiencing certain sensations or power dynamics, expressing other aspects of themselves, and a multitude of other elements.

Gender also has a huge impact on sexual roles and behaviour. One major example of this is the sexual double standard whereby men who are sexually active with several people are viewed positively, whereas women who do the same are viewed negatively. This is reflected in the English language in the fact that there are literally hundreds of words for a sexually active woman, almost all of them entirely negative, and just a handful of words for a sexually active man, all positive or neutral. Of course, as we've emphasised before, this is intersectional, with people of some race, class, or disability groups being assumed to be more sexually active, and more stigmatised for this, and others being assumed to be less so – or not sexual at all – and often being stigmatised for that too. When it comes to sexuality, women in particular are walking a fine line to be viewed as sexy enough without being labelled a slag or a slut.

The sexual imperative – the dominant cultural belief that it is 'good', 'normal', and 'necessary' to be sexual – also plays out in different ways according to gender. For example, often men are expected to be sexual – or to 'sow their wild oats' or 'play the field' – as a way of demonstrating their manliness through their sexual prowess. For women the imperative is often more to demonstrate their femininity through being desired by men and attractive to them. Many women also feel that they have to be sexual or run the risk of losing a relationship.

Finally, the sexual script itself is highly gendered. If you check out sex manuals and sex advice books, you'll see that 'proper' sex is often assumed to be PIV intercourse, with the majority of the books being devoted to different positions for doing this activity. When people fall into bed in Hollywood movies, this tends to be what they're depicted as doing too. Other forms of sex are often relegated to foreplay or regarded as being lesser than the 'real thing'. Of course only certain bodies are capable of PIV, and many of the ones that are capable of it experience far greater pleasure through other activities than that one – either all of the time, or on occasions.

A different approach

We follow sociologist Gayle Rubin[3] in calling for the dismantling of this kind of 'sex hierarchy' where one kind of sex is seen as superior to the rest, and replacing it with a vision of sex that is measured by how consensual and enjoyable it is to the people concerned, rather than how close it comes to some kind of 'norm' or 'ideal'. There's a lot more about how to go about tuning into your sexual desires, communicating them to others, and having consensual and enjoyable sex in the book that Meg-John wrote with sex educator Justin Hancock, called *Enjoy Sex (How, When and IF You Want to)*.

Let's turn now to a few people's experiences of how they've challenged dominant cultural assumptions about gender and sexuality, and the sexual script, in order to find their way to a gender, sexuality, and set of sexual practices that fit them better.

---

3   Rubin, G. (2013) 'Thinking Sex: Notes for a Radical Theory of the Politics of Sexuality.' In P.M. Nardi and B.E. Schneider (Eds) *Social Perspectives in Lesbian and Gay Studies: A Reader*, pp.100–33. London: Routledge.

Multiple experiences: Sex, sexuality, and gender

'Erotic fantasy and kink have been so helpful to me in exploring my gender. Initially I noticed that I could be a different gender in my fantasies and I found that really hot. I developed a dominant daddy role through fantasy, which was completely different to anything I'd experienced in real life. Through writing my fantasies down I could communicate about this with partners and potential partners. Eventually I found my way to a daddy-bear transmasculinity, which feels great for me in my sexual relationships and in my everyday life.'

'My husband and I had always bought into the standard heterosexual script, but to be honest it had never done much for either of us. We both kept at it, assuming it was what the other one wanted, until a drunken conversation when we were on holiday for our tenth anniversary! Now our default is mutual masturbation and we're both so much happier and more fulfilled.'

'I literally never enjoyed sex, but as a guy I felt like I ought to be doing it to prove my masculinity or something like that. Fortunately – or unfortunately – I could make my body work that way, but it was never good. Finally I discovered AVEN [Asexual Visibility and Education Network] online and it was like a revelation to me. I didn't have to have sex! I'm now in a great relationship with another ace guy.'

'There was always something missing in sex for me. I knew I was pretty active and confident sexually, compared to most women, and I would generally be the one to initiate contact, often getting on top to drive the whole experience. Somehow that wasn't enough. Then I was with this guy who shyly suggested I might want to explore pegging with him. I bought myself a strap-on and boom! I love it! It feels amazing to be the one doing the penetrating and controlling the other person's excitement in that way.'

'Our sex-negative culture did a real number on me. It defines "proper" sex as penis-in-vagina and that was never going to work for me because I hate being penetrated and can't come that way. I was so happy when I found more sex-positive communities, like the kink and poly communities. But then I found out there were a bunch of crappy sex assumptions there too: like you had to be doing it all the time, and with lots of different people, and trying all kinds of different things. In the end I took a step back from those communities as well, and tried to focus on just being me with the sexuality that I have, however fucked up they might all think that I am.'

Reflection point: Your sexuality and gender

What words do you use to describe your sexuality? You might want to think back to Sections 1 and 5 where we explored sexuality words and dimensions to some extent. How does your gender, and the gender of others, impact on the ways in which you view and name your sexuality, and the sexual practices that you engage in?

Are there aspects of your desire that you have expressed or not expressed because of your gender identity and expression? What would it look like to share aspects of your desires or sexual practices that have been unexpressed so far?

In Further Resources at the end of this section you can find links to a zine that includes lots of ideas for how you could make your own sex manual, or menu: a guide to your unique sexuality and the things that you do and don't enjoy.

REMEMBER: In addition to gender, our intimacy needs, relationship styles, sexualities, and sexual practices are also diverse. That's why some folks refer to it as GSRD (gender, sexual, and relationship diversity). If you'd find it useful, you could reflect on your sexuality and relationship style in much the same way in which you've reflected on your gender throughout this book. For example, you could do the following in relation to your sexuality and/or relationship style:

– Think about the language around it and how it is biopsychosocial (see Section 1).

– Reflect on how it is represented in wider culture, and how you relate to that (see Section 2).

– Consider your background in relation to it and how it has developed throughout your life (see Section 3).

– Explore its place in your life at the moment, and in relation to your other intersecting identities and experiences (see Section 4).

– Think about how you identify, name, express, and live it (see Section 5).

– Reflect on how you might communicate about it with others (this section).

– Consider whether to engage with communities, or seek out role models or support, in relation to it (see Section 7).

FURTHER RESOURCES

You can read about vulnerability in:

- Brown, B. (2103) *Daring Greatly: How the Courage to Be Vulnerable Transforms the Way We Live, Love, Parent, and Lead.* London: Penguin.

There's more about the politics of passing in the following book:

- Sycamore, M.S. (2010) *Nobody Passes: Rejecting the Rules of Gender and Conformity.* Emeryville, CA: Seal Press.

You can read more about the diversity of ways of doing relationships in the following books and websites:

- Barker, M. (2013) *Rewriting the Rules.* London: Routledge.

- www.rewriting-the-rules.com

- Barker, M.J. and Gabb, J. (2016) *The Secrets of Enduring Love: How to Make Relationships Last.* London: Penguin Random House.

- Taormino, T. (2010) *Opening Up: Creating and Sustaining Open Relationships.* San Francisco, CA: Cleis Press.

- Veaux, F. and Rickert, E. (2014) *More than Two: A Practical Guide to Ethical Polyamory.* Portland, OR: Thorntree Press.

- www.morethantwo.com

If you're concerned about the kinds of emotional abuse that we mentioned in this section, the following websites may be helpful in helping you to think it through and signposting you to supportive services:

- www.scarleteen.com/article/abuse_assault/blinders_off_getting_a_good_look_at_abuse_and_assault

- www.bishuk.com/relationships/abusive-relationships

- www.everydayfeminism.com/2015/08/worried-that-your-partner-is-emotionally-abusive-check-out-these-7-warning-signs

— www.telegraph.co.uk/women/life/my-friend-is-trapped-
in-an-abusive-relationship-how-can-i-help

If you want to read more about sex, then the following couple
of books might be helpful. The first one is more about cultural
assumptions and what's wrong with them. The second one is a
practical guide, similar to this one, but focused on sex.

— Barker, M.-J. (forthcoming 2018) *Psychology of Sex*. London:
Routledge and Psychology Press.

— Barker, M.-J. and Hancock, J. (2017) *Enjoy Sex (How, When
and If You Want to): A Practical and Inclusive Guide*. London:
Icon Books.

If you're interested in the relationship user guide, or sex menu,
mentioned in this section, you can get these from the resources
section on Meg-John and Justin's website:

— www.megjohnandjustin.com

The *Fucked* zines, about being sexually 'dysfunctional' in sex-
negative and sex-positive spaces, are incredibly helpful. You can
find information about them here:

— www.fuckedzine.tumblr.com

By now you're probably used to these 'breathe and slow down' pages. Still, we hope you found them as useful as we find any reminder to slow down in our daily lives.

Talking about sharing our genders with others, intimacy, close relationships, sex, and sexuality can be tough topics. You may have observed waves of thoughts, emotions, and sensations. Or you might find yourself a little spaced out, or numb.

Wherever you are, that's OK. Just notice, with curiosity and kindness, treating yourself with the same gentle care you would give a beloved.

Take some time to take care of yourself, whatever that might look like for you. We've given you some ideas throughout the book. Feel free to go back and check out the previous slow-down pages too, if you like.

Take time for YOU. What would it look like, in this moment, if you could meet some of your own needs? Do you even know what your needs are right now? Tune in and take care of this very important, primary, intimate relationship with yourself right now. When we can do this, we can also have more capacity to care for others.

You are worth your time, care, and attention. Your needs have worth. You can take time to nurture and care for yourself.

We'll say it again: You are worth your time, care, and attention.

After you have spent some time caring for yourself, come back, whenever you want, and the next section will be waiting for you.

SECTION 7

GENDER PIONEERS AND GENDER WARRIORS

Here you are in the final section of our book! By now you might have a better idea of where you are and where you've come from, in relation to your gender. This section is all about the fact that, wherever you find yourself in the gender landscape, you are not alone!

We've seen that dominant culture often takes an individualistic approach to everything, including gender, encouraging us to see ourselves as separate, atomised individuals who can be monitored, scrutinised, and compared against others. Our expression of our gender can be just one of those yardsticks with which we measure ourselves and measure others, and often find ourselves and/or others wanting.

But just as gender has a history and a culture, so do we as humans have all of these people who have identified and expressed their genders in diverse ways before us, who share our gender landscape at the moment, and who will come after we are gone as well. It's worth situating ourselves in this way, in time and space, and returning to the idea that we introduced in Sub-section 4.4: that we're all interconnected, including when it comes to gender. Many people find that identifying role models and engaging with communities are important ways of co-creating a livable life in relation to their gender. However, we'll also explore the ways in which role models, communities, and networks can close down options as well as opening them up, and touch on how we might deal with the pain and discomfort of tensions and conflicts within and between our gender communities.

This section is all about historical and contemporary examples of gender warriors and gender pioneers. It's a way to honour our ancestors as well as celebrating the current communities and individuals who pave the way for us, and our own role in this unfolding history of gender.

7.1 FINDING ROLE MODELS

Let's start with our own role models, in order to introduce you to some of the people who've inspired us on our gender journeys as well as giving you a sense of why having role models can be important. Given that gender is biopsychosocial, our role models around gender will be varied and appeal to different aspects of gender identities, experiences, roles, and expressions.

ALEX WRITES:

I feel my gender role models have changed over time, both as a reflection of my own growth and as an expansion of my own awareness. For example, feminist role models are the first ones I came across. The writing of Luce Irigaray impacted my sense of self as a teen, illuminating ways in which women were seen as commodities in dominant culture. Sibilla Aleramo's writing on life in the 1800s informed me of how women had been resisting patriarchy for a long time where I lived. Later I found the writing of Audre Lorde, Alice Walker, and bell hooks: writing that spoke to my soul not just of feminism, but also of culture, queerness, liberation, and resistance to gender-based violence. The musician Prince brought yet another dimension to my young self, with his gender-bending femme masculinity, which stirred parts of my identity and expressions.

In my twenties, thirties, and more recent years, other gender role models guided me through my own gender landscape, helping me to make sense of my thoughts, feelings, and experiences. People like Leslie Feinberg highlighted how transgender warriors have always existed, bringing new meaning to my long-standing love of Joan of Arc. Patrick Califia accompanied my explorations of gender and sexuality through the mazes of complex desires. Finally, more recently, my own gender education has been expanded by trans women of colour, such as Laverne Cox, Andrea Jenkins, and CeCe McDonald. CeCe, being local to where I live, has further expanded my compassion for what many trans women face when resisting systemic endorsed violence, especially when this is combined with racism. Andrea, also local to where I live but international in stature, just like CeCe, has moved my soul and activism to expand even further through her words and poetry. There are so many more role models I could mention here, such as S. Bear Bergman, Kit Yan, and Ignacio Rivera. I encourage you to look them all up through the power of the Internet! These are but a few beacons who illuminated key moments in my journey.

MEG-JOHN WRITES:

Like Alex, I've come to embrace different gender role models over time. Unlike Alex, I was well into my twenties before I was exposed to people who talked or wrote about gender. I'm ever-grateful to Jonathan Elcock, a colleague at my first academic post who didn't feel comfortable teaching the psychology of gender on his own as a guy. He roped me into joining him on the team and there started my quick and life-changing introduction to all things feminist and queer, as I nervously prepared to teach the course, only one step ahead of the students. Viv Burr, Ros Gill, Margie Wetherell, and Raewyn Connell were some of the authors who I particularly remember reading back then.

As a kid, a feminist friend of my family gave me one of Simone de Beauvoir's novels as a present. It looked intimidating and I never read it, eventually giving it to charity. What a mistake! When I finally read de Beauvoir in my thirties I found that she spoke to all of my own experiences, and helped me to think in more helpful ways about gender – and so much else. I also found her work a lot more accessible than that of her bff, Jean-Paul Sartre! Gayle Rubin, whom we mentioned in Sub-section 6.4, was another game-changer for me, as was Kate Bornstein, whom we've mentioned several times. Both of them showed me what a queer writer on the fringes of academia and activism could look like. These days I'm heavily inspired by Buddhist writer Pema Chödrön, who rarely addresses gender explicitly, but whose life and work help me when I view them through that lens. Sara Ahmed is another great inspiration, and her academic work around gender, race, and sexuality in current culture has had a major impact on my thinking. Unlike Alex,

I've come late in the day to black and intersectional feminists, but I'm finding them profoundly helpful now, especially when put into dialogue with Buddhist thought. The audio conversation between Pema Chödrön and Alice Walker is well worth a listen.

FIGURE 7.1: SOME OF OUR GENDER POSSIBILITY AND INSPIRATION MODELS

Different kinds of role models

So far, we've spoken mostly about role models who are celebrities and/or people who inform our thinking and activism. Let's touch on a few more types of role model before we move on.

Thinking back to Section 2, people who identified, expressed, or experienced their genders in diverse ways in the past can give us a sense of a gender ancestry, as well as a narrative back through time that can help us to feel legitimate in our current place in history. However, it's important to be careful not to read the past according to our present. We also need to be wary of viewing different cultural experiences through the lens of our own situation in simplistic ways that co-opt and appropriate them. Rather, it is essential to acknowledge both what we share and how we differ. For example, several different gender and sexuality groups see reflections of themselves in the Shakespearian boy players, or eighteenth-century mollies, but we must be cautious in claiming that they were 'really' the same as modern-day trans or gay people, given that gender and sexuality were understood in very different ways back then.

Closer to home, we may find people whom we actually know who encourage or support us in our gender journeys in some way. Meg-John already wrote in Section 4 about the importance, for them, of reading the blog of musician, scholar, and activist CN Lester, in terms of believing that it was possible for them to be openly non-binary, as well as Dominic Davies' role in helping them come to their current name. They might also mention their colleagues in both the Psychology of Sexualities and Psychology of Women sections of the British Psychological Society, who provided a supportive environment in which to develop as a queer, trans academic. Stuart Lorimer (psychiatrist at Gender Care) and Andrew Yelland (surgeon at Nuffield Health, Brighton) are worth mentioning too for being medics who were open and able to hear a non-binary gender narrative. And, of course, there is long-time collaborator, counselling psychologist Christina Richards, who opened up a long and ongoing dialogue about trans, which Meg-John might not otherwise have had.

And then there's the possibility of fictional characters as role models. The sci-fi and fantasy genres have a long history of imagining alternative universes and ways of being that open up gender possibilities, among others. Marge Piercy's *Woman on the Edge of Time*, Ursula Le Guin's *Left Hand of Darkness*, all the work of Octavia Butler, *Star Wars: The Force Awakens*, and odd episodes of *Star Trek*, *Red Dwarf*, and *Doctor Who* all provide ways of thinking about gender differently, which might help us to imagine an alternative gender future for ourselves. Meg-John has already spoken elsewhere in the book about the importance of male characters from *Buffy the Vampire Slayer* and *The Big Bang Theory* in their own gender role and expression. Additionally, John Watson from the Sherlock Holmes stories (in all their many incarnations) has also been an inspirational figure for them when it comes to their masculinity. There were many different reasons why they chose 'John' to be part of their name.

The importance of role models

Role models can be important for many reasons. Here's a summary of just a few of them (you may want to add your own):

- Through their work, or conversations we have with them, they can help us to think about gender in new and/or helpful ways.

- Through their lives they can provide us with models of diverse ways in which it's possible to live our genders.

- They can provide us with very specific gender options, such as taking on the pronouns they use, or similar clothing, hairstyles, or mannerisms.

- They can give us a sense that a livable life is possible in our gender – if we share aspects of it with them.

- They can give us a sense of legitimacy in our gender and be somebody (or somebodies) whom we can point to when people question us. We can say, 'Look, they're doing it too!'

- Through the ways in which their genders are different to our own, they can call us on our own assumptions, and encourage us into being better allies with others, such as the trans women and Black feminists in our examples.

- They can provide support when the going gets tough, either in person or through their teachings.

— Through their actions they can push us to think and act in ways we might not have imagined, as Meg-John's colleague Jonathan Elcock did, or inspire us in our own attempts to change the world gender-wise.

ACTIVITY: YOUR GENDER INSPIRATIONS

You may already know who has inspired you in your own gender journey or let you know that something was possible. Do something to honour this. For example, you could write them a letter – either one that you actually send, or one that you keep for yourself if it's not possible to send it or if you think that sending it might not feel consensual to them). You could make a collage of images of your gender inspirations. You could say 'thank-you' if it is someone in your social circle (or talk about how great they are in a book, blog-post, or zine – again, if you're sure that they'll feel OK about that).

If nobody springs to mind as being a helpful role model on your gender journey, do some research. You could follow up some of the people whom we've found helpful or some of the recommendations in 'Further resources' at the end of this section. Alternatively, you could think about people who are in the public eye or in your own social world – these could be people who inspire you right now or who might inspire you in your journey going forward.

In relation to all this, it's worth mentioning that, as with all things, role models can open some things up for us, and close other things down. (Remember this idea of opening up and closing down from Section 5?) As with communities, and other people in our lives, it's very easy to go into the idea of role models with a polarised view: either they are entirely good or they are entirely bad. There are several recent examples where people who've been a gender inspiration to many have been found to have behaved poorly at some point in their lives, and have been condemned completely for it all over social media. It's important to remember that if we put somebody up on a pedestal, it's a very precarious place for them to be. We're all human beings and that includes our heroes and queeros. Maybe, as with ourselves, we can simultaneously hold onto what's great about them and the ways in which they are inevitably imperfect.

Another related point is that, with our inspirations, it's worth remembering that we generally think a lot more about them than they do about us. That's why we've mentioned consent in the activity above. It can be tempting to reach out to one of our heroes to let them know how much they mean to us, but it may very well be that they receive many such messages and simply don't have time to respond to them all. Or we might catch them on an off-day. Or they may have tough experiences with stalkers and trolls and so are very cautious about replying to such messages. Don't be disappointed if you don't hear back or if a reply isn't the deep connection that you might have hoped for. Also, if there's a perceived or real power imbalance between us and them, that's not really a great basis for a real-life relationship (see Section 6 for more on relationships).

Reflection point: Inspiration or comparison

As you think about role models, we invite you to reflect on whether you compare yourself to them or whether you feel inspired by them. Notice the difference: inspiration tends to uplift us, whereas comparison tends to make us feel smaller and inferior. Gender role models are all about us feeling better in our genders, so it's best to go with folks who inspire us rather than our gender role models being a painful point of comparison.

7.2 FINDING COMMUNITY (IF YOU WANT TO)

We mentioned earlier that humans are social animals. There's an increasing amount of research that shows how we need other people in order to thrive and feel that we belong and are accepted completely for who we are. Safe and consensual touch is an important part of this for many. That's why so many professionals and community organisers advise parents of gender-creative children to just keep breathing when they're worried about their child's wellbeing, to keep loving them, and to be there for them. Research has shown us that family acceptance is a key protective factor for gender-creative and trans children and young people. Even the most introverted of us need some human contact, a sense of intimacy and belonging. Those who are more extroverted need more time with people than others do to thrive, and contact needs also vary with different forms of neurodiversity, but ultimately we all need some level of social connection.

These might seem bold statements to make in a book about gender. However, gender is but one multifaceted landscape that we navigate in our cultures, and this exploration cannot be disconnected from our interpersonal neurobiology – that is, what we know so far about our nervous system, including our polyvagal nervous system, which teaches us that we truly have a 'brain in our gut' too. Such knowledge reinforces the idea that we are socially connected beings. We need to be mirrored, validated, and recognised as who we are. For many of us, including those who may not fit into dominant cultural expectations of gender, whether in identities, expressions, roles, or experiences, this can mean finding 'our people'.

Who 'our people' are is, of course, a very subjective definition. For some folks, the whole of humanity might be considered their people. In our experience, there is usually a little bit of privilege behind such sentiments. When most of the people we see represented in mass media look like us, it might be easier to be swept up in 'all people are our people' sentiments. Of course it might also come from a non-dualistic view of the world and an authentic sense of connection with humanity. Determining who 'our people' are is no simple matter. We just want you to think about how our intersections and privilege might shape our views on this matter.

The intersections of our identities, together with dominant dynamics of power, privilege, and oppression, can make finding our people much more complex than it would otherwise be. We might share aspects of our gender identities, expressions, roles, and experiences with some people, but not others. We might feel as if we belong in one group of people or community but then experience feeling like parts of us are erased or diminished in those same places. For example, some aspects of ourselves might feel right at home in the bi community, whereas other aspects of ourselves, such as our ethnicity or class, might feel completely alienated or even oppressed within the same community. This can create painful experiences of feeling betrayed or 'othered' in communities and by people who are 'supposed to get us' because they are 'our people' in some way. We'll discuss some of these challenges further in Sub-section 7.3. Not everyone wants to find community, of course. In fact, many people, especially those who identify as trans and/or gender creative, might even feel fearful to be seen with other trans and gender-creative people. They might not want their identity conflated with one aspect or experience, such as being trans. Similarly, some women might declare loudly that they are not feminist, for fear of aligning themselves with values they find extreme or confusing. Some men might want to separate themselves from other men, in an effort to put distance between themselves and the patriarchy. Being part of a community might also make us feel like we are a larger target and that we cannot just hide and slip through the cracks, especially if we have the ability to do so.

There is no ideal 'one true community'. When we search for this, or think we've found it, there are many pitfalls, which we'll mention shortly. As with role models, it's important not to place communities on pedestals. We have observed that being on a pedestal can truly suck, as there is usually a longer way to fall when people realise we're all human and therefore fallible and prone to mistakes and differences. At the same time, living our lives openly can be an inspiration to others. The many people mentioned earlier are examples of this. As Laverne Cox said, when interviewed on the ABC show *Katie* (January 2014), maybe it's better to think of her and other people who live their lives openly as possibility models, rather than role models.

Finding, creating, and maintaining community requires quite a lot of emotional labour. We need to know when and where to invest time and commitment, when to stay, and when to move away. We're likely to make mistakes, and so are others. We don't need to like everyone we're in community with. In fact, being with people who always agree with us on everything can even be dangerous as it can lead to complacency and a sense that our way is the 'true way'. Community is also not only about validating us because we cannot validate ourselves. It can be helpful in this regard, but it can never be enough if we cannot find some love, acceptance, and compassion for ourselves. Community is just one piece of that puzzle.

It's impossible to give advice on how and where to find community for all of you readers, especially if your gender identities, roles, expressions, experiences, and intersections are as vast as we hoped and imagined them to be while writing this book. We invite you to revisit Section 6 and look at your intimacy needs, this time considering the social networks where those needs are met rather than just individual relationships. Where are the gaps, if any? What is it that you need more or less of in your life? Below are some examples of lived experiences to support your reflections.

Multiple experiences: Finding community

'I will never forget my first, national bi community event. There were so many people there, of all genders, sexualities, and expressions. There were masculine women, effeminate men, trans and gender-fluid people, straight, gay, and lesbian partners of bi people, and children as well! So many ways of being! I remember watching people dance on the Saturday night and realising that I get to be whoever I want to be. I get to be queer and look however I want. Maybe I even get to decide what my gender is, instead of having to listen to what other people tell me. It was all very liberating.'

'Thank goodness for parenting groups! I don't think I would have survived the first year of my baby's life if it wasn't for the mom support group I was sent to by my doctor. I'm not exaggerating. I was very depressed after the birth of my child. My partner had left me while I was pregnant, my family lives a long way away, and I really didn't know how I would have coped without these other women in my life. They helped me get out of the house when I wanted to shut myself in. They laughed and cried with me. They helped me cook when I couldn't face it. They were there for me, and slowly I managed to be able to be there for them too. Our kids are in high school now but we're still all tight friends. I'm so grateful to them.'

'I kept going to trans support groups because my therapist told me to. I hated it. Week after week I tried. I felt people were too political there. I was just trying to live my life, hold onto my job, my sanity, my family, and friends. I didn't want to talk about the gender binary. I wanted advice on where to shop, where to swim safely, how to talk to my teenage son. I didn't feel there was space for that there. Eventually I formed a couple of close friendships online with other trans people and felt much happier this way, meeting people one-to-one and talking about our everyday lives.'

'My faith community is essential to me. I found a place to worship where I feel more comfortable with my own idea of divinity, and where I feel accepted as a Black person and as a lesbian. They are my main support. That's where I go every week, during all major religious holidays, when I feel sick or tired, when I am heartbroken or full of joy. I cannot imagine not having a place like that, and the people who go there, in my life. It's a lifeline. Their presence in my life supports my activism and my work in the world as a community organiser.'

'Everyone told me I should find community, or support groups, when I came out as a gay man. I didn't want to. I had plenty of male friends who accepted me for who I am. Sure, most of them are straight, but that doesn't matter to me. We watch sports, drink beers, and complain about our partners. We're just guys, hanging out. I really don't get what all the fuss about community is about. I don't feel lonely and I don't know what I would have in common with other gay guys, apart from being gay.'

'Finding and nurturing relationships with other Two-Spirit people has been essential to my sense of self. I am so glad we decided to organise in our region. Sure, we come from many different Indigenous people and traditions, but we also have so many shared experiences and beliefs. We honour the Earth, we honour each other, we honour our ancestors, and believe in our families, and working consciously for our descendants. I don't have to explain myself. I don't have to fit in with expectations that make no sense to me. We come together. We share time and food, we talk about what matters, we support each other.'

**Reflection point: Networks
and communities**

Take a moment to think some more about the social networks and communities you belong to. Which networks are you part of? How does your gender impact your participation in those networks? Are there networks you would like to be part of or create? If so, what are they? How would being part of, or creating, those networks impact your life moving forward? Are you happy with the social networks in your life? If not, what is missing? If so, what do you appreciate most about them?

7.3 COMMUNITY: SUPPORT AND TENSIONS

As we described in Sub-section 7.2, you don't have to find a community. Many of us, however, will experience a range of communities over time. For example, as children we might experience being part of a school or home-schooling community, being part of a playgroup, or being involved in an organised interest group such as scouts or guides. We're likely to move between communities as we grow and as the sense of ourselves shifts and changes.

We've already visited the idea (in Section 3) that we're not born into a gender-neutral landscape, as far as our families of origin are concerned. Our families have their own generational and intergenerational stories, including gender stories. Similarly, our communities form within larger sociocultural, economic, and political stories of gender. When looking for 'our people', we're making a dualistic distinction from 'other people' (i.e. those who are not our people). When it comes to gender, our ideas about who we view as being 'our people' or not might be based on our understanding of biology, on psychological traits, or on social experiences. None of these are neutral, which makes things even more complicated. For example, if we only consider genitals as part of our biological component of gender, we are missing out on other biological aspects of gender, such as our chromosomes and our brains, which are also essential parts of our biological make-up! As humans, we frequently and automatically make distinctions between 'people like us' and 'people not like us'. This is partly connected to our need to recognise who and which situations are safe, and which are not. However, this also means that many of us have painful moments of being told we don't belong somewhere. When these moments happen in the early years and/or in relation to people who are core to our survival and wellbeing, such as parents and caregivers, they can leave a lasting impression, and influence how we feel about ourselves and how we approach others.

Trauma and community

One way of describing these kinds of moments can be through the lens of trauma. Trauma can be interpersonal and directly experienced. It can also be historical, social, and cultural. For example, in the United Kingdom and the United States, trans and gender-creative people come into a cloud of historical, social, and cultural trauma, already enshrined in legal systems, relational patterns, and even in architecture (e.g. public restrooms and changing rooms). Even though it might seem most evident for trans people, we also believe that all of us come into that cloud of gender trauma, although we might be differently impacted, depending on our position in the gender landscape.

We've already addressed how rigid binary ideas of masculinity and femininity can be toxic for our wellbeing, regardless of gender identity. As we interact with the dominant cultural ideas of gender and with each other, we're also moving in, and are touched by, this cloud of historical, social, and cultural trauma. At the same time, we're shaped by the intergenerational gender stories in our family, and in a circular way, by our own interpersonal experiences of gender, where we might also have experienced pain. For example, a Two-Spirit Indigenous person reclaiming their gender and sexuality is also struggling with the violent legacy of settler-colonialism and the destruction of cultural, linguistic, and spiritual practices that recognised and honoured their experiences.

When we differentiate between those who are 'like us' and those who aren't, we're trying, to some degree, to protect ourselves. There can be many ways of protecting ourselves by dividing into groups. We might fight fiercely, for example, to maintain a certain definition of 'women's only' spaces or to protect gender divisions in league sports. We might ignore, erase, or freeze out of our spaces those who we feel don't belong there. We might also consider those who don't belong with us as belonging to the categories of those who are against us. This might then lead us to fight even more fiercely to keep those people out, as they're seen as oppressors and threats to our safety and wellbeing.

When we feel our safety and wellbeing are threatened, we tend to go into survival mode. In this mode, as social animals, we want the pack to stay together and either we hunt the predator or run away from it. We might feel that opening up, being vulnerable, and sharing our pain and fears makes us easy prey. We might also feel that opening up to listening to the pain, fears, and experiences of those we consider to be 'not like us' could diminish or erase our own pain, fears, and experiences. Can we still honour our own pain and trauma if we experience compassion for the pain and trauma of others, especially those we view as part of the group of people that caused us pain in the first place? What would that open up and what would it close down?

A social and historical example of this is second-wave feminism. Both of us came into fairly binary ideas of gender, and into a time where women's studies was a discipline that didn't refer to all women but rather to people who were assigned female at birth. Alex, for example, spent some time teaching in this area, and, while doing so, tried hard to make peace with his body as it was. He felt that not accepting his body and femininity must be due to the patriarchy and a symptom of internalised misogyny. Therefore, for a long time, he felt that accepting their womanhood was an essential part of the healing process. He eventually realised that having made peace with his sex assigned at birth didn't mean having to live as a woman if that's not who he was. This didn't seem too problematic. There was a level of acceptance for masculinity among people assigned female at birth due to the belief that our biology and socialisation gave us common ground. While honouring the women's-only spaces that were conducive to much of his healing, Alex also started to realise that many women's spaces were not accessible to, or accepting of, trans women. In this current historical moment, those second-wave feminist spaces are often protected by what has been named trans-exclusionary radical feminism, commonly referred to as TERF.

TERF views are particularly impactful for trans women and feminine people, even though they also negatively impact trans men and masculine people. They view trans women as essentially male, reducing their identities, roles, and experiences to their genitals at birth. Conversely, they view trans men as really women who are so damaged by the patriarchy that they embrace a male identity. It's particularly painful to witness the level of hate, attack, and rejection aimed at trans women for many of us who were shaped and brought up by second-wave feminists in our personal, professional, and community lives. It seems clear to us that people holding onto TERF positions are scared of letting trans women into their circles in case this erases their own painful history and experiences. However, by doing so, these views further reinforce patriarchal, misogynistic views that basically reduce women to their genitals at birth.

This is but one example of how we might go into a fight, flight, or freeze response when faced with the challenge of determining who belongs in our communities. This challenge is deeply shaped by dynamics of privilege, power, and oppression, and is not new. In the 1980s, bell hooks challenged White feminism with her book *Ain't I a Woman*. There have been waves of conflict in feminism around who is included and who is excluded in the definition of 'woman' before and after this time. Similar conflict is present in many communities.

In trans and queer communities, for example, there are often narratives about who is 'really' trans and/or queer. Many people struggle with not feeling 'trans enough' or 'queer enough' as they measure themselves and each other with the yardsticks of judgement and division. For many of us who have felt threatened and lost friends and lovers to hatred and violence, making those divisions, however, might seem essential to maintaining the integrity and safety of our communities.

This means that building and maintaining community can be extremely challenging on individual and collective levels, especially when we're trying to build communities centred around gender – an area where many of us have experienced individual and collective historical, social, and cultural trauma. There can be reactivity in individuals and groups, meaning that people easily withdraw or lash out. This can make it difficult to build trust and relationship through authentic vulnerability. Community intimacy might simply seem a risk too large to take on.

Nurturing resilience and support

Let's take a breath. We might have painted a rather bleak picture in the last few paragraphs! While we want to be realistic, and acknowledge that community is not all about rainbow ponies, glittery unicorns, and allergy-friendly ice-cream of all kinds, we also want to acknowledge the strength, resilience, and support that communities have provided, and continue to provide, for us. Trauma is most certainly an issue that cannot be ignored when talking about gender and community-building, but so is resistance.

Across all those difficulties and challenges, people continue to find their way to each other, to expand categories and make room for one another, to heal from the toxic messages of dominant culture, to fight alongside each other, and to build communities, again and again. Being social animals definitely helps with this. We might be afraid and defensive, but we also long to connect with others, and to have people on 'our side'.

Building community, in our experience, means investing enough into our relationships so that we can start to listen to each other, appreciating the range of our experiences and moving beyond the irritations and reactivity we might sometimes experience. Do we have tools to recognise when our nervous system has been triggered and we're in fight, flight, or freeze mode? Can we recognise when we're dissociating, putting our stories onto others, fighting for our lives, or wanting to leave? Can we take care of our nervous systems so that, once soothed, we might approach the situation, other people, and ourselves with curiosity and kindness?

Many of us build community around common goals, or even common 'enemies'. Depending on our intersections of identities, our lives and those of the people around us might be threatened on a daily basis. There's an urgency to change things, to keep each other safe, and to work harder than ever because the work is vast. These are real issues. However, we also need time to take care of ourselves and each other, to heal, to rest, to grieve, and to come together.

Colonisation, consumer capitalism, and White supremacy want us to believe that we're alone, that we're never enough and can never do enough, that we need to work harder and be perfect, and that our minds rule our bodies.

Gender liberation and community-building are also about resisting those messages. Can we move back and say no? Can we name our differences and challenges, holding them with open hands, trying to find ways of resolving conflict that do not reinforce normative cultures?

Both of us have witnessed moments in offline and online spaces where reactivity can flare up into a forest fire if we're not willing to take some breathing room and space to align our intention more closely with our impact. Online spaces, such as social media, are particularly explosive as there is vital information missing from our interactions, including each other's physical presence. Also, people might not seem as 'real' in online spaces and we might say things that we would never say to someone's face.

We want to clarify that we're not saying that one way of expressing ourselves is better than another. Alex, for example, has experienced plenty of tone-policing in Anglo spaces, especially when upset, as his emotions tend to be very transparent and easily read on his body. This is something that some Anglo folks see as a direct attack and experience as a trigger. It is a fine dance of mindfulness: respecting other people's experiences, hurt parts, and sensitivities, while also staying true to ourselves, our own hurt parts, and identities. The more differences there are between us, the more mines we might set off inadvertently, if we're not willing to listen to one another and broaden the horizons of our awareness.

We still maintain that this is a dance worth engaging in, as the support and resilience we might find in community cannot be found in individual isolation. We want to conclude these sentiments with some words from Black trans woman actor and activist Laverne Cox:[1]

> Each and every one of us has the capacity to be an oppressor... I want to encourage each and every one of us to interrogate how we might be an oppressor, and how we might be able to become liberators for ourselves and each other.

Reflection point: Knowing our own reactivity

Take a few moments to consider the following questions: Where do you find yourself being the most reactive with others in community, that is, those moments that 'make your blood boil' or when you want to run out of the room, or find yourself numb or frozen in place? Can you recognise that impulse to fight, run away, or freeze? How do these feelings manifest in your body? What are the sensations, thoughts, feelings, images, stories, and behaviours that arise in these moments for you? What are the ways in which you soothe your nervous system, that is, come back to a more neutral space where you can hold conversations more intentionally, maintaining curiosity and presence?

---

1   Excerpt from Laverne Cox's speech at the GLAAD 25th annual Media Awards in Los Angeles, 2014.

And breathe…

We're almost at the end of this book. Of
course you can come back as many times
as you think it might be useful, but, for
now, we're reaching the conclusions.

You may want to take this opportunity to think
about support you might have experienced in
your life. Where did that support come from?
Was it from people, characters, books, films,
nature, or songs? Was it simply your breath,
always there, in and out? Was it the ground that
supported you even when you were crumpled and
tired and maybe feeling defeated and alone?

Whatever it is, if you want to, take a few
moments to express your gratitude for the
support you received. You can do this by writing
in your journal or notebook, through drawing,
movement, song, or silence. Take as long as you
need to and spend some time with gratitude.

If you cannot think of any time you felt supported,
take some time to go back to your breath.

Remember, you can always come
back to your breath.

Breathe in, breathe out. In… Out… In… Out…

Here you are. You're perfect and whole,
as you are, in this moment. It's OK if that
doesn't feel true. Let yourself imagine it
might be, even if for a fleeting moment.

Breathe in, breathe out. Here you are. And
you're not alone. Others have lived in this vast
gender landscape before you, and others will
live in the same yet different landscape.

You're not the first and you won't be the last.

Breathe into gratitude for a few more
moments, and into the support of your
breath and the support of gravity.

Then, when you're ready, let's carry
on for just a little bit longer.

7.4 CHANGING THE WORLD!

We touched already in Section 5 on how our reflections about our gender can risk turning us inwards instead of outwards. Our self-monitoring culture encourages us to always be internally scrutinising ourselves: trying to figure out whether we're normal and, if not, how we can fix ourselves; whether our appearance is up to scratch; whether we're successful enough, popular enough, or happy enough. We saw in Sub-section 7.3 that even when we find communities outside of society's gender norms, they frequently have their own versions of this. We can find ourselves trying to measure up to some new norm of the 'good gay citizen', measuring whether we're queer enough, assessing how well we fit the dominant trans narrative, or trying to figure out whether our body fits some perceived ideal of androgyny.

There's a danger, if our gender journeys stay entirely on the internal, personal level, that they can reinforce this self-critical way of being in ourselves, and in the others around us who see us treating ourselves in this way and perhaps follow our lead: our friends, colleagues, parents, partners, kids, and so on.

Throughout the book we've endeavoured to keep inviting you to turn outwards as much as inwards, pointing out that our genders are situated in history, in the wider world, in our relationships, and in our everyday contexts.

Outward focus is also a great way to resist the shaming, criticising, judging culture that we live in. We can gently but firmly point out that if our genders are difficult in our place and time in history, then it's the world that's flawed and needs to change, not us. Without this approach we might never have reached the point of gender equality we're at now, because women would have simply focused on how to make themselves more feminine – according to patriarchal standards – instead of embracing feminism and demanding equal rights. Similarly, LGBTQ+ people might still be being imprisoned and treated with drugs or electroshock therapies, instead of occupying the place they currently do in many countries as equal citizens with heterosexual and cis people.

It's important to remember, however, that 'turning out' in this way is not just about obvious forms of activism such as taking to the streets, engaging in politics, or writing a book. These things are not for everyone by any means, and we need diverse forms of activism to change the world, many of which may be far closer to home. As always, it's vital to recognise the role of power and privilege here. It's simply a lot safer, or more possible, for some people to engage in certain forms of activism than it is for others.

Here are a few examples to give you an idea of the range of things that people can do.

Multiple experiences: Diverse ways of changing the world

'In my school we were getting sick of the way boys were always twanging girls' bra-straps or making sexual comments. We mentioned it to a teacher, but all we got was an assembly about how we shouldn't wear short skirts – like it was our fault! At that point, a bunch of us did an art project about sexual harassment and how the focus is always on girls to change their behaviour, instead of on the boys who are actually doing it. We also started challenging the boys on social media when they were saying those things. I think everyone's finally getting the message now.'

'All my life I thought I should be doing certain things to make the world a better place. I tried being a teacher in an inner-city school, like the one I went to, and briefly working with young offenders to help them find a different path. It turns out I'm pretty terrified of teenagers and not so great at that kind of work! Now I run a retreat centre where lots of activists, therapists, youth-workers, and so on come to recuperate, to run groups, to write, and to make things. By creating that space, I like to think I'm helping them to make a difference in the world, and that's pretty valuable too.'

'My main form of activism? Parenting. I'm making sure that my kids grow up knowing about diversity, thinking critically, and feeling OK about themselves. In the world we live in right now that's a radical act.'

'I have this rule on social media that I always wait at least an hour before responding to somebody's post or comment, and then I always try to find the most compassionate way of responding that I can. I try to think about where the person writing might be coming from and what their vulnerabilities might be, and then I try to respond in the way that I think they might be able to hear. It doesn't get across to them every time, of course, but sometimes it does and that feels amazing. It generally leaves me feeling a lot better than when I just used to cut people down when they said something that I disagreed with. And I hope it shows other people that there are different ways of behaving on social media.'

'As a therapist and trainer, self-care is actually my most important form of activism. I used to run around doing a million things and burn myself out. Now I take on far less. I make sure I take time out at the start of each day so that I always begin my work in a calm place. I also write my journal for an hour before seeing clients, and I make sure that I get my own therapy. I think a lot about surrounding myself with supportive people to help me through the more challenging aspects of my job. It's made a world of difference, and also means I'm a better role model for my clients and trainees.'

'The moment that sticks in my mind is: I was working on some roadworks with a bunch of guys. This young woman walked passed and they were all cat-calling her. I could tell they were making her really uncomfortable. I totally lost it with them and told them to shape up. Like how would they feel if it was their sister or daughter being treated in this way? They didn't do it again – at least not when I was around!'

'I never thought of myself as an activist. I'm just a maths teacher. Then one kid in my school came up to me and told me that having an openly trans teacher had made it feel OK for them to come out as being trans. It took me till I was 43 to tell people I was trans. It meant the world to know that I'd had a role in at least one other person not having to wait that long.'

In these examples you can see that we're often not even aware of the ways in which we're impacting on the world around us. Also the small things that we do can end up having a big effect, far wider than we realise. We're reminded of the story of the teachers in Cornwall, in the United Kingdom, who found that they had a trans kid in one of their classes. They looked to find some information about what they should do to best support them and could find no official policies. So they got together with teachers from other schools in the region and worked with experts on trans to develop their own. Now their guidelines are mentioned in national governmental reports as good practice.

You've also seen mentions of compassionate activism and self-care here. Compassionate activism is when we recognise all of our capacity to be both oppressor and oppressed, and try to engage people who are being oppressive in ways that they might be able to hear: perhaps ways that could reach us if we were being oppressive and felt defensive about it. This is sometimes called 'calling people in' rather than 'calling people out'. Call-out culture often involves publicly shaming people, which can be incredibly destructive, adding to the shame that most of us already feel. Calling in recognises that we're all imperfect but that we can learn, and it also acknowledges the dynamics of privilege in play in who has access to the most up-to-date terminology and ways of speaking about things, for example.

Self-care is another extremely helpful idea from Black feminist Audre Lorde. She famously said: 'Caring for myself is not self-indulgence, it is self-preservation, and that is an act of political warfare.'[2] In relation to gender and its intersections, we can see self-care as a radical political act in many ways, such as the following:

- It can keep us alive when oppressive messaging from dominant culture makes us feel we would be better off dead.

- It radically counters the approach of self-criticism, which is so prevalent in wider culture and in our institutions, communities, and families, providing us – and others – with an alternative option.

- It means that we have more energy to care for others.

---

2   Lorde, A. (1988) *A Burst of Light: Essays*. Michigan: Firebrand Books. See also: www.bitchmedia.org/article/audre-lorde-thought-self-care-act-political-warfare, accessed on 8 June 2017.

– Through cultivating kindness for ourselves it's easier to see other people's vulnerability (beneath their defensive attacking or withdrawing behaviours) and to treat them kindly.

– It puts us in a more grounded place to make informed decisions about what we do and where we put our energy.

– It makes it more possible to face up to our own capacity to hurt others – intentionally or unintentionally – so that when it happens we don't lash out or burn out, and can take responsibility for our actions.

This is partly why we've included so many invitations to you to care for yourself over the course of this book. You might find it useful to reflect on what forms of self-care you build into your daily life and what other ones you may like to incorporate. It is very hard – if not impossible – to care for others, to respond compassionately to people who have different views, and to have energy for community organising or activism if we do not build communities with ethics of care.

ACTIVITY: WHAT YOU DO ALREADY

Take a moment to breathe and really recognise that the ways in which you identify, express, and experience your gender have an impact on the world around you. If this is difficult to do at first, don't worry. Maybe think about your typical week or month, or the last year in your life. Is the *impact* of the way you live in line with your *intention* or not? If not, what things might need to shift for you?

Remember to go gently when making such changes – it's not about fixing what's wrong with you or correcting flaws; rather, it's about gradually noticing what works well and less well, and intentionally and gently moving towards what works better.

Reflection point: Our impact

Think about your role in your circles of intimacy as well as in the broader world. Who do you think is impacted by your gender identity, expressions and experiences, and who are you impacted by? What are the ripples you create? What are the ones that create the waves that lift you up and down?

REMEMBER: Before concluding, we want to end this final section in the book with a further quote from one of our own favourite gender pioneers, Laverne Cox:[3] 'As long as we are living in a culture where one has to prove their womanhood or manhood, we are not living in a free culture.'

---

3   Excerpt from Laverne Cox's speech 'Ain't I a Woman: My Journey to Womanhood'. Available at www.youtube.com/watch?v=iKOVXsMbvWQ, accessed on 8 June 2017.

FURTHER RESOURCES

Amelia Bayes's zine *Hot Topic* is all about different people's (gender) role models. You can pick it up here:

- www.etsy.com/uk/listing/268480807/hot-topic-2016-idols-and-inspirations?ref=shop_home_active_4

An excellent book that explores the potentials and challenges in current gender communities – particularly feminist, trans, and queer communities, is this:

- Serano, J. (2013) *Excluded: Making Feminist and Queer Movements More Inclusive.* New York, NY: Seal Press.

You can read about Serano's other work on her website:

- www.juliaserano.com

As we've mentioned in this section, it can often be really useful to read other people's gender stories. The two gender outlaw books below give lots of different people's stories of their relationships with gender:

- Bornstein, K. (2013) *Gender Outlaw: On Men, Women and the Rest of Us.* London: Routledge.
- Bornstein, K. and Bergman, S.B. (2010) *Gender Outlaws: The Next Generation.* Berkeley, CA: Seal Press.

In addition to the wonderful Kate Bornstein – who put these books together – S. Bear Bergman is another gender hero of ours, and his books are well worth checking out if you enjoy funny, gentle, moving, real-life stories about gender and much more.

- Bergman, S.B. (2009) *The Nearest Exit May Be Behind You.* British Columbia: Arsenal Pulp Press.

Some other useful autobiographical accounts around gender include the books by Laurie Penny and Jack Urwin that we mentioned at the end of Section 2 (as well as Laurie Penny's other excellent work). We also recommend:

– Jacques, J. (2015) *Trans: A Memoir*. London: Verso books.

– Lester, CN (2016) *Trans Like Me: A Journey for All of Us*. London: Virago.

– Mock, J. (2014) *Redefining Realness: My Path to Womanhood, Identity, Love & So Much More*. New York, NY: Simon and Schuster.

– Moran, C. (2012) *How to Be a Woman*. London: Harper Perennial.

– Strauss, N. (2005) *The Game: Penetrating the Secret Society of Pickup Artists*. London: HarperCollins.

– Vincent, N. (2006) *Self-Made Man*. London: Penguin Books.

The latter three books are by no means unproblematic, but they do provide a fascinating insight into various experiences of femininity and masculinity.

You can read more about gender in the following books:

– Burr, V. (2002) *Gender and Social Psychology*. London: Routledge.

– Connell, R.W. (2014) *Gender and Power: Society, the Person and Sexual Politics*. Hoboken, NJ: John Wiley & Sons.

– Edley, N. and Wetherell, M. (1995) *Men in Perspective*. London: Pearson Education.

– Gill, R. (2007) *Gender and the Media*. Cambridge: Polity.

We actively encourage you to find your own possibility models and inspiration. Here are some we have appreciated in case they could be helpful starting points:

– Califia, P. (2002) *Speaking Sex to Power: The Politics of Queer Sex*. Jersey City: Cleis Press.

– Crenshaw, K. (2018) *On Intersectionality: Essential Writings*. New York, NY: The New Press.

- Feinberg, L. (1998) *Trans Liberation: Beyond Pink or Blue.* Boston: Beacon Press.

Ignacio G. Rivera is a storyteller, artist, writer, activist, and educator. You can find out more about their written work at:

- www.ignaciogrivera.com/it-is-written.html

Kit Yan is a playwright, performer, poet, and lyricist and you can find out more about Kit's work at:

- http://kityanpoet.com

S. Bear Bergman is a writer, educator, and storyteller and you can find out more about him at:

- www.sbearbergman.com

Andrea Jenkins is a poet and you can find out more about her at:

- http://andreajenkins.webs.com

Reina Gossett is an activist, writer, filmmaker, and artist and you can find out more about her at:

- www.reinagossett.com

Mikki Kendall is a writer of fiction and non-fiction. You can find out more about her at:

- mikkikendall.com/about

Publication details of work by some of the other writers mentioned in the text are as follows:

- Ahmed, S. (2017) *Living a Feminist Life.* Durham, CA: Duke University Press.

- Butler, O. (2004) *Kindred.* Boston, MA: Beacon Press.

- Chödrön, P. (2000) *When Things Fall Apart: Heart Advice for Difficult Times.* Boulder, CO: Shambhala Publications.

- Chödrön, P. and Walker, A. (2014) *On the Meaning of Suffering and the Mystery of Joy.* Boulder, CO: Sounds True.

— De Beauvoir, S. (2014) *The Second Sex*. London: Random House.

— hooks, b. (1987) *Ain't I a Woman*. London: Pluto Press.

— Le Guin, U.K. (2012) *The Left Hand of Darkness*. London: Hachette UK.

— Piercy, M. (2016) *Woman on the Edge of Time*. London: Random House.

If books aren't your thing, there are some great art projects, capturing something of the diversity of bodies and styles that are possible across gender in photographs and other art forms. A couple of examples are:

— www.identityprojectsf.com

— www.genderportraits.com

The everyday feminism website has links to the ideas of compassionate activism and self-care, or self-love:

— www.everydayfeminism.com

There's a piece by Meg-John and Jamie Heckert about oppression and privilege conversations here:

— www.sociologicalimagination.org/archives/6520

You can read more about self-care here:

— www.blackgirldangerous.org/2015/05/more-than-self-care-cultivating-joy-in-our-lives-ask-bgd-1

— www.feministkilljoys.com/2014/08/25/selfcare-as-warfare

CONCLUSIONS

We're not sure how much more we have left to say on this topic and, by now, you may be looking forward to putting down this book and taking this journey in your own direction. So we won't be spending too much time drawing conclusions, especially as they will likely be different for each reader. At the beginning of this book, we discussed that gender is a complex biopsychosocial construct. This means that gender impacts every facet of our identities, roles, expressions, and experiences. We also discussed how gender intersects with all these other aspects of our identities, such as ethnicity, language, class, spirituality, disability, and more.

We truly believe that knowing our own gender stories, including how they have changed and continue to change over time, is important for everyone. We also talked about how the world has its own gender stories across time and space. Things that now seem to be 'just the normal order of things' have not always been this way. Gender has many histories across time and space, and it continues to do so. The story of gender is a living, breathing, ever-evolving story because it is *our* story. We are part of the history of gender.

You reading this book, living your life, and expressing yourself are ways in which you are engaging with the flow of that story!

When you picked up this book, you were already in that flow, whether you were aware of it or not. Our hope is that this book has been a companion on your journey. By now, you have reflected on your own gender origin story, that is, how your gender was perceived when you came into the world and how that was dependent on so many factors: your family's gender stories, your culture, language, age, ethnicity, spirituality, and so on.

You have also taken a substantial amount of time reflecting on your current gender, not just as an identity but also in relationship to how you express yourself in different places, with a range of people and at various times in your life. You have considered gender too in relationship to roles and experiences across your lifespan so far. During all of this, you have also been invited to consider your relationship to ideas such as the gender binary, which is one of the current popular models of gender where we live.

You may have decided that the way you identify and express your gender right now feels comfortable, or you have decided to make some changes. You may have had conversations about your gender with people around you. Some might have gone well and others less so. Hopefully the supportive experiences have outweighed the negative ones. We dream of a world where people of all genders can feel supported and safe. That world can feel like a fantasy on most days!

We hope that you have identified your own gender warriors, pioneers, and possibility models. We also hope that you have found (or are working on finding) community, whether it is online or face to face. For us, finding connection, representation, and community has been an essential part of our journey. It also continues to nourish us as we face a world that is often not supportive of our own gender identities, expressions, roles, and experiences, and of those of our clients, family members, and communities. We have written this book because we ultimately have a strong belief that every one of us is essential. We do not need to be special, but we do believe we are all essential. This means that your story, your gender, your experiences matter. We need all of us to work towards liberation for all of us. Therefore, in some ways, writing this book is also an act of self-preservation. You are essential to our liberation. We are woven into a web of interdependence, and the more present, aware, and in relationship with one another we can be, the better we can figure out how to collaborate in making this world safer and freer, every day. So, from our hearts to your heart, thank you for taking this journey with us. Thank you for exploring the history of gender and your part in that story. Thank you for allowing us to share this part of the journey with you. We sincerely hope this book has been a resource for you and/or others in your life – a resource you can come back to and share with others, as needed.

Reflection point: Your gender journey continues

We have asked you to engage in reflecting on your own story at various points in this book. Now that we are at the end of the book, we are asking you one more time to pause and reflect. Journal, make art, or share a conversation with someone to reflect on how you feel after reading this book. Having read it, how will this inform you moving forward? Who are your allies and accomplices in your gender journey? Who else might benefit from this resource, if you are ready to pass this book on?

Index